D0743516

Seasonal Affective Disorder Treatment

Since Humans Shouldn't Hibernate

Jozzie Ray

The Happy Sun

Chesapeake

Copyright

Seasonal Affective Disorder Treatment

Since Humans Shouldn't Hibernate

Jozzie Ray

Printed in the United States of America
First Printing, 2015
ISBN: 978-0-9966434-0-5 (Paperback)
Editor: Brendan Dabkowski
Cover Design: Jozzie Ray

Publisher:
The Happy Sun
Chesapeake, VA

For publishing inquiries email:
TheHappySun@yahoo.com

Disclaimer

This book is published for the purpose of general reference only and is not intended to be taken as substitution for independent verification by the reader. Although the author has made every effort to ensure that all the information contained in these pages was accurate at the time of publishing, the author and publisher do not assume and hereby disclaim any liability to any party for any loss, damage, or disruption caused by anything including (but not limited to) errors or omissions, whether such errors or omissions result from negligence, accident, or any other cause.

The material in this book may include information, products, or services by third parties. Third Party Material consists of the products and opinions expressed by their owners. As such, the authors of this guide do not assume responsibility or liability for any Third Party Material, products or opinions. External links may be affiliate links that could result in the author receiving compensation when you traverse the link. Due to the nature of affiliate marketing you will be directed to the merchants own website when you click on an affiliate link. This means that you will end up on exactly the same website and see the same result regardless of whether you visit the merchant's website directly yourself or reach it via an affiliate link. You will pay the same purchase price for goods and services, so passing through an affiliate site will have no direct impact on your purchase at all.

Regardless, the only products or services recommended are those which I believe will add value to my readers.

I am disclosing this in accordance with the Federal Trade Commission's 16 CFR, Part 255: "Guides Concerning the Use of Endorsements and Testimonials in Advertising." The publication of such Third Party Material does not constitute the authors' guarantee of any information, instruction, opinion, products, or services contained within the Third Party Material. Publication of such Third Party Material is simply a recommendation and expression of the authors' own opinion of that material.

Whether because of the general evolution of the Internet or the unforeseen changes in company policy and editorial submission guidelines, what is stated as fact at the time of this writing might become outdated or simply inapplicable at a later date.

This book is not intended to provide medical advice or to substitute for the advice of a personal physician. The reader should consult a physician in matters relating to one's health and particularly with respect to any symptoms and conditions that might require diagnosis or medical attention. It is in no way the intent of the author to diagnose or prescribe. Many health care professionals hold a wide variety of views on the subject of this book. The author and publisher disclaim any liability arising directly or indirectly from the use of this book. The sole purpose of this book is to offer information to help you work with your physician in a cooperative manner.

Table of Contents

The Who, When, and Where of Seasonal Affective Disorder 25

"The Who" and Who does SAD affect? 25

When: SAD Through the Years 26

Mama Bears 27

Let's Hear it For the Boys 29

SAD Children 31

Does Your Child Have ADHD or is it SAD? 32

SAD Symptoms in Children 33

Sundown Syndrome in the Elderly 36

Shift Workers 37

Where: It's a SAD World 38

Why Do I Have Seasonal Affective Disorder? 41

Let There Be Light 42

Genetic Mutation in Eye 44

Circadian Rhythms 44

Neurotransmitters and Hormones 46

Melatonin and Serotonin 48

Amino Acid Tryptophan and The Miracle of 5-HTP 50

Dopamine and Norepinephrine 51

Amino Acid Tyrosine 52

Dedication

For all of us who

suffer from *sunshine withdrawal symptoms*

and the friends and family who support us

even when we are SAD

...especially my family.

Introduction

Introduction...or Perhaps a Warning

I started writing this book last year. Ironically, I noticed recently that I never finished it. My apologies. I have a medical condition that inhibited my progress. It's a genetic predisposition to human hibernation, which resulted in a total loss of motivation on my part. This condition is called Seasonal Affective Disorder, **or SAD, for short, if you are simply too tired to spell out the whole thing.**

Random Author's Comment:

Before we go along any further in this literary adventure, you should be warned that the author's first language is actually sarcasm. Despite the opinion of my many childhood teachers, I believe it is my most endearing characteristic. However, in an effort to separate the science from the sarcasm I will do my best to indicate sarcastic comments with either (parentheses), italics, or in a specific area like this clearly labeled "Random Author's Comment." Now that we are on the same page (literally), let's get back to this SAD topic.

Chances are you have heard about Seasonal Affective Disorder, SAD, or the Winter Blues. You probably already have a good idea whether you might even have this condition (which would be my educated guess on why you purchased this book). After all, we live in the information age and, thanks to the Internet, have become extremely adept in the art of medical self-diagnosis.

A Quick Word of Caution

You do need to be careful with all this self-help medical advice on the Internet or you could become a "cyber-chondriac." Similar to a hypochondriac, or someone who is constantly convinced that he or she has some type of serious medical condition, a cyberchondriac is basically a more educated version of the classic hypochondriac thanks to all the information floating around in cyberspace. (But, hey, without all that great technology this gem of a self-help book would not be available for your reading pleasure!)

I should insert some type of legal disclaimer here as well stating that this book is not intended to replace any type of actual medical advice. I am not a doctor. (Becoming a physician requires lots of schooling, and I may have dropped out of college *for some strange reason* in late November one year.)

Suicide Hotline

If you are feeling seriously depressed or suicidal, please call your physician or, if you live in the United States, 1-800-SUICIDE (1-800-784-2433) now. Sadly, we have lost family and friends whose depression ultimately lead to suicide. There is hope. Pick up the phone and let someone know how bad you are feeling. *Please let someone help you.*

Why Such a SAD Book?

I wrote this book to provide a little more insight, explanation and entertainment about the topic of Seasonal Affective Disorder. Most of the blogs, articles, and books I have read regurgitate and recycle the same information in a similar manner. (You will find out later in this book that many people with SAD might also have another popular acronym, ADHD, and people with Attention Deficit Hyperactivity Disorder and may become *slightly* bored sifting through this information.) My goal is to elaborate on the causes of and treatments for Seasonal Affective Disorder from my own somewhat humorous perspective, and hopefully make you laugh a little and learn a little too.

There are many scientific references in this book (in addition to high levels of sarcasm). Since I was a teenager, I've had a strong to desire to understand **why** I struggled so much with depression in the winter. SAD has always had a drastic impact on the quality of my life. I had often heard of depression simply explained as a "chemical imbalance in the brain." I needed to learn **what brain chemicals** were unbalanced and why. I was driven to truly understand the science behind what was causing SAD, so I could in turn understand **how** certain treatments worked. **I discovered that when I truly understood *why* a treatment was effective, I was more apt to actually follow it.**

This began my love affair with "brain books." I will admit that I am far behind on my reading of popular romance novels. For more than 25 years, I have read and reread hundreds of books on brain chemicals (and wondered why my friends had no interest in exchanging books with me or inviting me to book clubs). I have searched the Internet and read *or attempted to read* medical studies and scholarly articles on SAD, many of which are referenced at the end of this book. I have tried to summarize and organize this information, added my own personal trials and errors and created a sort of Seasonal Affective Disorder survival guide for you. It is my hope that my journey and perspective might offer a little more enlightenment to those "living a SAD life".

The truth is our brain chemicals have a drastic impact on us. They affect our moods, thoughts, and feelings, and they impact our behaviors. When our brain chemistry is in balance, we feel more in balance in our daily lives. We have a good level of energy and can handle the obstacles and stress in our lives reasonably well. When our brain chemistry is off, life can feel very overwhelming and we can struggle with even the smallest tasks. I have learned that optimizing my health provides me with options and choices. I will never be perfect; I will always have challenges that I struggle with, but having balanced brain chemicals allows me to handle life with reason and not overwhelming emotion.

In my reading, I also realized that the same chemical imbalances in the brain that cause Seasonal Affective Disorder also cause other ailments. As you will learn, there is a connection between Seasonal Affective Disorder, ADHD, alcohol and drug issues, and other conditions. Correcting the underlying imbalance will often help many of these other issues in addition to SAD. Too often we tend to look at medical conditions as if they are a singular issue, without backing up to examine the individual as a whole and what other issues may be related to the root cause.

End of Chapter Mystery Links (EBook Only)

If you do, in fact, have that ADHD tendency, I have offered you an alternative method to read this book. The beginning of the book has a nice organized Table of Contents, which a typical person would read in order. As I mentioned, I read a lot. I have noticed that I have this bizarre habit where I almost never read a book in order. I often jump from chapter to chapter (or even book to book) to read whatever strikes my interest at that moment.

As somewhat of an experiment, I thought it would be fun to offer an ADHD Mystery link at the end of each chapter in the EBook version of this book. The link will bring you to a random chapter within the book. The point is to get you all the way through the book, but just not in the structured order of the table of contents. The goal is to hold your interest by trying to present the information in an innovative way. Some of the information might not make sense since you didn't read the previous chapter, but I thought it would be a fun way to read this book anyway.

Let's begin. If you want zigzag throughout this book in a disorganized fashion and have the Ebook, click on the Mystery Link now. If not, simply turn the page (as Bob Seger would say).

<u>Mystery Link: Jump to a Random Chapter</u>

You Might Have

Seasonal Affective Disorder if

Let's just go over the basic symptoms of SAD to make sure you that you have correctly diagnosed yourself and that you are in fact are reading the right book.

You might have SAD if ... you truly wish humans could hibernate for the winter.

You might have SAD if ... you have no clue how Santa's elves could be jolly at the North Pole.

You might have SAD if ... your metabolism gets "laid off" every winter and stops working completely.

You might have SAD if ... your entire winter wardrobe has elastic waistbands, also known as "sweat pants syndrome."

You might have SAD if … in the winter your sex "drive" screeches to a halt like a deadlocked traffic jam.

You might have SAD if… the 50 shades of gray in your life refers to the color of the "dirty" snow outside your house.

You might have SAD if … you carb load like an elite marathon runner but are a serious contender for the winter Olympic gold medal in marathon napping.

You might have SAD if … you secretly wish you were older … like, old enough to retire in Florida.

You might have SAD if … you would willingly kill the groundhog with your snow shovel given the chance.

You might have SAD if … dead people actually have warmer hands and feet than you do.

You might have SAD if … you have secretly devoured the bulk of your children's Halloween candy while they were at school and then lectured them on why it is not healthy.

You might have SAD if … you have called in sick to work by explaining the truth … that your bed possesses a strong magnetic force preventing you from getting out of it.

You might have SAD if … you hope to get a tan from the headlights of passing cars while driving to and from work in the dark.

You might have SAD if ... you have tried to pull off wearing a Snuggie at your company holiday party.

You might have SAD if ... you love your summer sandals so much that you are considering attending a "Flip Flops Anonymous" meeting.

You might have SAD if ... your vitamin D levels are lower than a vampire with osteoporosis.

You might have SAD if... you are physically detoxing from "sunshine withdrawal syndrome."

Finally you might have SAD if ... you are attempting to get *free light therapy* by staring at your neighbor's over-decorated Christmas light display.

If you can relate to most of the previously listed symptoms, well then you might have Seasonal Affective Disorder. Since you have done a good job of medical self-diagnosis, keep reading and let's see if we can make your life a little brighter! *Congratulations on buying the right book!*

Have a Funny Description of Your SAD Life?

We would love to hear it!

Share it with us and find other SAD friends on our "You Might Have Seasonal Affective Disorder if" Facebook page at

http://Facebook.com/YouMightHaveSeasonalAffectiveDisorderIf

What is

Seasonal Affective Disorder?

In case you have not already scoured the Internet, let me cover the basics about *what* Seasonal Affective Disorder is. We will review the "standard list of symptoms" as well as "my personal list of symptoms" based on my own life experiences. For example, my list includes dropping out of college and "sweat pants syndrome" as signs of SAD.

Standard Description of Seasonal Affective Disorder

Seasonal Affective Disorder, also known as SAD, is a type of depression that follows a seasonal pattern. The depressive symptoms occur around the same time every year, typically in the late fall or winter months and then subside in the spring. It is also commonly referred to as the "winter blues" or "winter depression."

The personalities and behaviors of people suffering from SAD transition with the seasons. People with SAD tend to be moody, tired, and depressed during the winter. The depression then subsides, and they feel happier again when the sun becomes stronger in the warmer months.

Spring and summer often bring about a renewed quality of life, and some SAD suffers tend to become manic or hyper during this time of year. The seasonal pattern or trend of depression is what differentiates SAD from other types of depression.

Some people are mildly affected by the winter blues, while others with Seasonal Affective Disorder experience a true winter depression. The severity of the symptoms and how they affect a person's quality of life are the differentiating factors between a case of the winter blues or Seasonal Affective Disorder. The predictable pattern of reoccurring and diminishing symptoms over a period of years differentiates SAD from other types of depression.

Medical Definition of Seasonal Affective Disorder

Since a physician will not diagnose you based on my personal definition (probably, again, because I am not a physician) let me take a moment to discuss the "official" medical definition of Seasonal Affective Disorder.

Seasonal Affective Disorder is a recognized medical condition by the American Psychiatric Association and is recorded in the Diagnostic and Statistical Manual of Mental Disorders (DSM IV).

It is not listed as its own separate mood disorder, but rather defined as a "specifier," or type of classification, of major depression in the DSM IV. To be diagnosed as having SAD, one must first meet the definition of having depression and then the seasonal pattern is factored in.

A physician diagnosing SAD would look for a pattern of the onset of depressive symptoms during a specific time of year followed by a full remission at a later time of year. Physicians look for this pattern of seasonal symptoms for at least two years to meet the clinical definition of having Seasonal Affective Disorder. There would be no other social or psychological reasons for the depression, other than the change of season.

An online dictionary sponsored by Merriam-Webster lists the definition of Seasonal Affective Disorder as "depression that tends to recur as the days grow shorter during the fall and winter."

Standard List of SAD Symptoms

Seasonal Affective Disorder is often overlooked or goes undiagnosed. (Perhaps this is because so many of us are great at diagnosing ourselves thanks to the Internet!) Many people do not understand that SAD is a medical condition, with a biological cause, and instead tend to rationalize away or minimize the impact SAD has on their lives.

For an accurate diagnosis, it is important to discuss the seasonality of the depression with your physician. Each person might exhibit different symptoms but repeatedly experience a seasonal pattern of depressive symptoms including the following:

- Irritability and Mood Swings
- Decreased energy
- Weight gain
- Fatigue and a tendency to oversleep
- Sleep disturbances
- Night wakings (common in children with SAD)
- A change in appetite
- Increased cravings for sweet and starchy foods
- Difficulty concentrating
- Problems in school for children with SAD
- Avoidance of social situations
- Lack of interest in activities or hobbies
- Lack of interest in sex

My Description of SAD

If you have not done so yet, go back and read my version of "You might have SAD if... " It really is the heart and soul of this book and a rather humorously accurate description of living with Seasonal Affective Disorder.

Human Hibernation

Apparently it is socially unacceptable for humans to hibernate for the winter. It is seemingly impractical to quit my job, drop out of school, end all my relationships and responsibilities for an entire season each year *despite my best attempts to do so.* It is also equally impractical for most of us humans to migrate to and from northern and southern homes, depending upon the season. While I aspire to be a retiree (or a bird) with the ability to do so, I needed to come up with an interim solution for my SAD urges to hibernate or migrate. Thus the birth of this book.

No one likes feeling exhausted, miserable, and irritable. Friends, family, and co-workers do not enjoy being around grumpy bears who rather hibernate either. I am pretty sure you cannot rationalize a bear out of hibernation by simply explaining to the bear that it *shouldn't be* so tired in the winter. Even if you justify to the bear that other animals don't hibernate so it shouldn't either, the bear will most likely ignore you and head to its cave for a long winter nap. It is biologically engineered to do so, despite all reason. Yet we seem to think that we can explain, rationalize, justify, or ignore our SAD.

The reality is that Seasonal Affective Disorder has had a drastic impact on my life and who I am as a person. My depression has resulted in lost friendships, failed relationships, and family dysfunction. It has also affected my educational and career choices, as I dropped out of college and have changed jobs impulsively. SAD has made it difficult to make healthy choices, resulting in weight gain and other health concerns. Seasonal Affective Disorder is part of my biology, and it drives and influences my motivation and behaviors. To put it bluntly, *I am living a SAD life!*

Transition Weeks

After years of self-evaluation, with both successful and failed attempts to improve upon my life and health, I realized that Seasonal Affective Disorder affects my life not only in the winter but throughout the entire year as well. There are a few weeks between the transition from summer to fall and also between the winter and spring that are generally intense, for lack of a better word.

Personally, I know I can begin to feel the changes in myself starting as early as August each year. The back to school commercials are on in full swing and every retail outlet is anticipating a new school year complete with center aisle bins loaded with pencils and notebooks. I try to enjoy the cool change in the weather and the autumn activities, but I am slowly starting to struggle.

I tend to freak out when the back-to-school ads come on TV. I can't help it. Friends and family assure me there still is plenty of good weather left before winter arrives. They think I am overreacting, but my body and brain are amped up. It is my "nut gathering season." I start panicking about the upcoming winter ... and literally going nuts.

The month of September usually brings about a sense of restlessness and irritability. There is a primal urge to change something drastic in my life. I want to flee or escape. It is compelling desire comparable to the instinct of a bird to migrate south for the winter or a squirrel to start gathering nuts. My panic season generally last for a few weeks, and then I fizzle out and settle into a winter funk. By Halloween, I have officially lost my battle and settle into my zombie like state of existence shuffling around in the darkness.

I also noticed how amazing I feel as the snow melts away and the sun is starting to feel strong and warm again in the early spring. I seem to have an intense amount of positive energy and ambition during this transition time. I am ramped up and ready to start living again.

I have a history of ending relationships in the fall and finding love in the spring. I begin hobbies in the spring that I quit in the fall. The ebb and flow of the seasons have affected my motivation and influenced my life decisions deeply. It just took me awhile to see the patterns of my behavior, and realize what was happening.

Becoming aware of my seasonal patterns was a huge step in my life. Once I started to accept that these are my natural patterns and tendencies, I was able to try to work with them instead of unrealistically fighting against them. (I was also able to warn my then-boyfriend, now-husband, that I would probably attempt to break up with him in the late fall, but to wait me out a few weeks and I would settle down again. Luckily for me, he waited me out and continues to do so from year to year.)

There are positive attributes to having Seasonal Affective Disorder as well such as "spring fever" and the strong possibility of being highly creative. (Hey, I finally wrote this book after all!)

Spring Fever

Most of what I have found to read about SAD focuses on the depressing winter symptoms. However, spring and summer often bring about a renewed quality of life and some SAD suffers tend to become hyper or even manic during this time of year. I do feel that "spring fever" is an under-discussed positive attribute of having Seasonal Affective Disorder.

While I truly would rather hibernate for the winter, I become extremely extroverted and highly productive in the spring and summer. I tend to be efficient and am able to accomplish many things. To some degree, I think this helps compensate for my sloth-like pace in the winter.

In the spring I am bursting with life, full of ideas and creativity. I am ready to clean, declutter, and organize my house and my life. This is the time of year that I will paint or redecorate rooms and declutter closets. I will admit that I *occasionally start too many projects* at once and *might* inadvertently make more of a mess of things than actually organize them, but hey I am trying to make up for lost time in the winter.

I tend to plan social events and host parties in the summer. I clean up my diet and exercise routine. Simply put, I am full of love and laughter during my peak season. These are the good qualities of Seasonal Affective Disorder. While my friends who do not suffer from SAD are more reliable and stable throughout the year, those of us with SAD can be the life of the party during the spring and summer and achieve many goals.

It can take people years to realize the seasonal pattern of their depression. Since everyone has bad days or time periods in their lives, people might not always make the connection between having Seasonal Affective Disorder and their symptoms and behaviors. They might not realize that their life patterns ebb and flow with the seasons. When looking back over a time period, it might be easier to see the pattern from behavior.

Highly Creative

Interestingly, this mood cycling pattern also tends to be linked with individuals who are highly creative (except when they are hibernating for the winter). Kay Redfield Jamison has conducted some fascinating studies linking mood cycling and seasonal patterns to the work of artists, writers, musicians, and other highly creative individuals. You may suffer from Seasonal Affective Disorder, but there is a pretty good chance that you might be highly creative too.

"Besides, balance is boring," says the ADHD in my brain. In upcoming chapters we discuss the links between Seasonal Affective Disorder and other related medical issues such as ADHD and Bipolar Disorder.

My overall point here, however, is that having Seasonal Affective Disorder does have some positive effects on our lives and can be indirectly attributed to producing some amazing works of literature, art, and music!

The poet in me would describe SAD in the winter as

"The shortage of sunlight is slowly suffocating my soul."

~Jozzie Ray

While the summer version of myself might agree that this is a little bit of an *overdramatic* description, the winter version of myself feels that this description is spot-on accurate. (Yes, KR Jamison, I wrote that analogy in the fall.) While in the spring or summer, I would describe SAD in a much more light-hearted manner such as

"I was genetically engineered for summer.

I was born barefoot."

~Jozzie Ray

My List of SAD Symptoms

After having read and reread the standard list of Seasonal Affective Disorder symptoms many times over the years, it occurred to me that my SAD symptoms were directly reflected in my life events through the years. I have also come to realize that the spring didn't just diminish the depression but also brought forth a second set of behaviors or symptoms as well.

My Fall / Winter SAD Symptoms:

- Constantly tired and cold
- Decline in grades and performance in school
- Dropping out of college
- Ending relationships
- Quitting diet / exercise routine
- Feeling like I had little control over what I ate
- Constantly being hungry and eating poorly (despite good intentions)
- Secretly devouring kids Halloween candy
- Gaining weight (for some reason?!?)
- Fruits & vegetables become unappetizing
- Quitting or being fired from a job
- Sweat Pants Syndrome—Living in sweatpants
- Missing the ending of all your television shows (from falling asleep on the couch too early)
- Difficulty getting out of bed in the morning
- Never finishing projects (such as this book)
- Major procrastination
- Wanting to stay home all the time
- Not returning calls, text messages, or emails
- Skipping social events, especially in evenings
- Brain fog—Drifting off while in the middle of ...
- Irritated with family and friends

- Total apathy- too tired to care about anything
- Negative attitude
- Complaining about people, places, and things
- Easily annoyed by my children
- Frustrated with mess in my house
- Crying easily
- Lack of food in the house (too cold/dark to shop)
- Doing as much shopping as possible online
- (Thank you Amazon.com!)

My Spring / Summer SAD Symptoms:

- Starting new exercise routines
- Eating healthier
- Fruits and vegetables taste better
- Starting a new job / Receiving a promotion
- Starting a new hobby
- Needing little sleep
- Falling in love
- Redecorating the house
- Major decluttering and cleaning
- Lots of Shopping
- Drinking more alcohol
- Becoming much more sexually active
- Becoming very creative
- Highly motivated and able to multi-task
- School detention (too many sarcastic comments)
- Arranging social gatherings
- Bursting with ideas and life

What is YOUR List of SAD Symptoms?

Take a minute to reflect back on your life. Think about some of the major life decisions you made or possible regrets you might have. What month did these events occur in your life?

When did you last change jobs? Do you notice any advancement in your career tied to increased motivation levels in the spring? Looking at your resume, is there a seasonal pattern for you involving job changes?

What month did you start dating the person you are with? Or what month did you break up with the last person you were dating? What month did you get married? Is there a seasonal pattern for you involving relationships?

When were you very successful at doing something? When did you decide to quit or give up on something you were working toward? If you play a musical instrument, do you notice whether there is any seasonal pattern with your desire to play? Are there any creative hobbies you are drawn to more during certain seasons?

Do you give up on dieting and your health during the winter but try to turn over a new leaf in the spring? Do you notice increase shopping patterns and or that you may be spending money in the spring?

Think back to your childhood. What was school like for you? Can you remember experiencing similar feelings back then? Do you see these patterns reflected throughout your later years in school or college? Did you finish school?

Do you see these patterns in other family members you are genetically related to? Parents? Brothers? Sisters? Children?

Do you think Seasonal Affective Disorder might possibly have a greater impact on your life other than simply feeling blue in the winter?

The Who, When & Where of

Seasonal Affective Disorder?

"The Who" and Who does SAD Affect?

While it has been reported that members of the band The Who have suffered from depression, the goal of this chapter is to focus more on the people "who" seasonal affective disorder affects. In an attempt to keep with journalistic integrity, I aim to also cover in this chapter the "when" and "where" of SAD in the chapter also.

Unfortunately, we do "know what it is like to be the SAD man" and "to feel these feelings—like I do." That classic Who song, "Behind Blue Eyes," does has some more chilling lyrics that could potentially reference SAD: "If I shiver, please give me a blanket. Keep me warm—Let me wear your coat." Enough with The Who feeling blue; let's look now at *who* SAD affects.

Who does SAD affect?

The American Academy of Family Physicians estimates that six percent of the population suffers from Seasonal Affective Disorder. It is estimated that an additional 10% to 20% of the population has a milder version, or what is commonly called the winter blues.

I have read that statistic many times previously, but while editing this book I became curious and visited Wikipedia. Wikipedia, in turn, references the U.S. Census Bureau, which estimates that there are more than 7 billion people in the world. If six percent of the world's population suffers from seasonal affective disorder, that equates with approximately 420,000,000 people who suffer from SAD worldwide! If you estimate that 20% of the world's population gets the "winter blues," that equates with approximately 1.4 billion who feel blue during the winter! Wow!

There is also a strong genetic link, meaning that seasonal affective disorder tends to run in families. *Having multiple family members feeling tired and irritable during the winter can make for some "interesting" family holidays.*

When: SAD Through the Years

Studies indicate that largest demographic that Seasonal Affective Disorder affects tends to be women between the ages of 20 and 30. This research also suggests that the average age of onset for SAD is somewhere between 20 and 30 years old. It is my opinion that this information might be somewhat skewed. There is actually a larger population including men, children, and the elderly whose lives are greatly affected by SAD, but the disorder may be under diagnosed or under reported.

It has been my experience that SAD symptoms can be exhibited differently among these demographics. Many people with Seasonal Affective Disorder recall experiencing the effects of changing seasons throughout their childhood. Also men do tend to experience depressive symptoms differently than women and can be less likely to seek professional help.

Let's delve a bit more into the "who" and "when" of seasonal affective disorder, and examine how SAD might play out through the years as symptoms might evolve. Since we are demographically popular, we will start with "Ladies first!"

Mama Bears

The age that many women are diagnosed with Seasonal Affective Disorder tends to between 20 and 30 years old. It is thought that the reason for this has to do with the natural shift in female hormones that occur between these ages. In addition to hormonal fluctuation, it is between these ages that many of us become Mama Bears. Mama Bears are infamous for putting too many expectations on themselves and attempting to get everything in the world done at once.

There are varying degrees of severity of SAD, and the symptoms can become more severe and noticeable during this age span. My worst year was when I was 30 after I had changed jobs—in the fall. My old office had two bright windows, and my new office came with an overwhelming amount of stress, an atmosphere characterized by poor training, and one window—facing north—that was always in shadow. Every single day felt like an endless exhausting struggle. Each endless minute of that winter felt like an eternity.

If you are a mother with SAD, you might also have children who were born in the winter. Nothing like that spring solstice to boost your fertility like a rabbit! Spring sunshine makes you feel happy and in love. Physically, your body functions more efficiently. Ironically, it is this spring romance that often tends to produce babies who are up all night in middle of the winter—exactly when you, as a parent with SAD, want to sleep the most.

My son was born in February, and less than two years later my daughter was born in January. Postpartum hormone shifts do *NOT* help with Seasonal Affective Disorder either. I had a few very tough winters when my babies were still babies. My almost 2-year-old son decided to give up napping the month after his sister was born. He liked to wake up at 5:30 a.m. every day, despite the fact that his sister was up all night. This was not an enjoyable experience for this Mama Bear. I was more than exhausted not just from parenting, but also from my winter depression. I was truly happy to be a new parent and tried to keep a positive attitude during that special time.

Honestly, it was a very difficult time. I physically felt awful and was so sleep-deprived I think I was temporarily transformed into an actual zombie. I apologize if I inadvertently started that zombie apocalypse trend. I was spotted in public places, such as at the grocery store, in my zombie-like condition. I was seen shuffling along with dark circles under my eyes, dragging the unwilling bodies of toddlers with me while attempting to gather food. Zombies like potato chips ... and sweat pants.

Moms: Cut yourself some slack for feeling bad, and get the help you need to take care of yourself!!! Seriously, if you have even mild postpartum depression and Seasonal Affective Disorder, please see your physician and be honest about how you are feeling. I advocate pursuing many natural remedies in this book, but with the double combination of fluctuating hormones and unbalanced brain chemicals you might need at least temporary medical intervention. I tortured myself unnecessarily by trying to "tough it out" and keep a positive attitude during that time in my life. I should have listened to friends and family and let the doctors help as I was an obvious train wreck... or a zombie that was in in a train wreck.

Let's Hear it for the Boys

Men and boys do get SAD too. My son exhibited symptoms of Season Affective Disorder when he was as young as 5 or 6 years old. (I might have been too tired to notice them earlier.) Symptoms of the disorder in men and boys might be expressed a little

differently than in women. Women tend to be more
outwardly weepy (and bitchy) than guys. Women
might also discuss their feelings more.

Guys tend to complain more about physical aches and
pains rather than their moods when feeling depressed.
Headaches, stomach issues, and joint pain are
common. Self-esteem and confidence issues often
manifest by men expressing dissatisfaction with their
jobs. Guys tend to escape more through electronic
devices, withdrawing from the world and their
families. Obsession with a new hobby can also actually
be a symptom of male depression, according to
PsychCentral.com. An increase in the use of alcohol or
drugs can make it difficult to determine whether the
issue is the booze or whether the drinking emerged
from an underlying depression.

If you have a man in your life who is exhibiting these
symptoms, try to realize that his behaviors might be a
symptom of an underlying brain chemical imbalance.
Men can feel better when they restore their brain
chemistry. They might not even realize how much of a
funk they are in. With Seasonal Affective Disorder,
these same guys might bounce back to life in the
spring and never notice their own patterns or trends.
Rather than judging their behaviors or demeaning
them, educate the men in your life on male depression
and encourage them to seek help.

Unfortunately, men also have a higher rate of suicide
than women. There is a startling trend of men in their
20s taking their own lives. There is a secondary trend
of older men in their 60s also committing suicide.
These men get to a point physically and mentally
where they feel so bad that they just want it to stop.

Perhaps they have tried unsuccessful treatments in the past, but, sadly, many of these men have never asked for help. There is help. Please call, or have them call, 1-800-SUICIDE (1-800-784-2433) and seek professional medical help.

SAD Children

Though the disorder is not easily diagnosed in children, many adults with Seasonal Affective Disorder can trace their symptoms back to childhood. Since symptoms often start showing up in late fall and early winter, SAD children often struggle in school. Their renewed energy in the spring also tends to make these kids hyperactive, which can cause behavior problems in school. Children with Seasonal Affective Disorder might actually be diagnosed as having Attention Deficit Hyperactivity Disorder ADHD. There is a strong link between SAD and ADHD. Seasonal Affective Disorder also has a genetic link and tends to run in families.

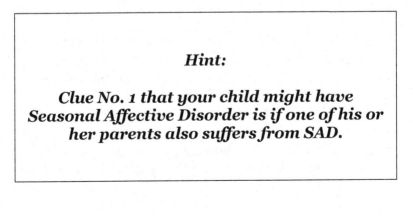

Hint:

Clue No. 1 that your child might have Seasonal Affective Disorder is if one of his or her parents also suffers from SAD.

I can recall having symptoms of SAD as a child and teenager. I am sure this is why I quit my high school basketball team, despite it being my favorite sport. I mean, who really wants to exercise after school while it is dark when you can go home and take a nap? Yawn.

Likewise, my hyperactive behavior in the classroom during the spring was not greatly tolerated by my past teachers. During my high school years, I often had detention conflicts, as multiple teachers attempted to hold me after school on the same day. I occasionally would need to reschedule my detentions to future dates due to these detention conflicts. (Apparently no one appreciated my "talent" in sarcasm until now.)

As a side note, I always hated the lighting in schools and think improving the quality of lights might aid many children's ability to focus and learn.

Does Your Child have ADHD, or is it SAD?

Especially in children, Seasonal Affective Disorder symptoms are commonly mistaken for Attention Deficit Hyperactivity Disorder ADHD because the onset of their depression follows the school year. The two conditions are often seen together, because similar biochemical imbalances in the brain cause both the conditions. Following is a list of questions to ask in order to determine whether your child might be experiencing SAD or ADHD:

Are you experiencing behavior problems with your child?

Is your child having issues in school?

Do teachers and professionals encourage you to test your child for ADHD?

Are you concerned about putting your child on medication?

Has your child dropped out of activities he or she once enjoyed?

Is your child having sleep issues or disturbances?

Do you notice cravings for sugary foods and carbohydrates in your child's diet?

SAD Symptoms in Children

Mood Swings and Behavior Problems

All children can be moody or irritable, but for children with Seasonal Affective Disorder there is a distinct pattern of these behaviors developing and continuing during the fall and winter months. Temper tantrums, crankiness, and obvious lack of energy can be clues that a child is struggling with Seasonal Affective Disorder.

Changes in Sleep Patterns

In adults, SAD suffers are generally tired and tend to oversleep. In children, sleep disturbances can manifest differently. Such disturbances might include frequent night wakings and difficulty falling asleep. This can be a very frustrating battle for parents.

Problems in School

Children with SAD often have problems in school due to their symptoms. Difficulty concentrating and lethargy might impede a child's ability to complete his or her necessary tasks. It is often a teacher who will notice these difficulties with a child, but the teacher might not necessarily recognize the seasonal pattern. This can often lead to a misdiagnosis of ADHD.

Diet and Cravings

People struggling with depression often turn to food to try and compensate for their chemical imbalances. In essence, people with SAD are trying to "self-medicate" by eating increased amounts of sugar and carbohydrates. Children with SAD are no exception and can crave sweets, starchy foods, and other carbohydrates.

Diagnosing SAD

Because SAD symptoms generally start in late fall, they literally follow the school calendar year. Since teachers generally don't see students during the summer, the remission of symptoms may not be observed. Because the symptoms of SAD escalate as the school year progresses, it can often be confused with Attention Deficit Hyperactivity Disorder ADHD, as the seasonal pattern may not be recognized. This can create some confusion for parents and physicians resulting in difficulty in obtaining an accurate diagnosis of Seasonal Affective Disorder in children.

As parents, we often think the solution is to become more stern or strict with our children when their behaviors become unruly and punish them. The reality is that our brain chemicals control much of our moods and, in turn, drive our own behaviors. When children don't feel well, they act out. You cannot correct brain chemical imbalances by arguing with your children or punishing them. If we can help children correct their own biochemical imbalances, they will feel better and, in turn, behave better.

The treatments discussed later in this book, can also benefit children. Melatonin—which is available over the counter in both pill and liquid form—can help children suffering from night wakings or who have difficulty falling asleep. It comes in a liquid form as well. 5-hydroxytryptophan (5-HTP) has been known to help with mood and irritability issues associated with SAD in children, and this supplement also comes in a quick-dissolve formula for children who cannot or will not swallow a capsule. Light therapy is also an effective treatment to help children with Seasonal Affective Disorder.

There is often a hereditary link with Seasonal Affective Disorder. Knowing that a parent, sibling, or other close relative has SAD can prove valuable to your pediatrician.

Sundown Syndrome in the Elderly:

Don't Let the Sun Go Down on Me

Anyone who has worked in a nursing home knows exactly which patients have sundown syndrome, or sundowning, as it is also called. It generally affects patients with Alzheimer disease or dementia. These are the sweet patients who get agitated and confused around the time when the sun goes down or shortly after the 3–11 p.m. shift begins.

Such patients often cannot sleep, and the 11 p.m.–7 a.m. shift knows these patients well too. They often wander the halls in a confused manner, sometimes looking for an obscure object from their past that has meaning to them. "I can't find my red purse! Someone stole my red purse!" said the 89-year-old woman dressed in her best clothes at 9:50 p.m. They can become angry or combative if you try to redirect or help them in this confused state, especially after they realize it was probably *you* who stole the purse.

If you are trying to care for an elderly family member at home, sundowning can be a major factor in caregiver burn-out. Some of the same treatments for Seasonal Affective Disorder have been known to help these patients, which is good news for *my personal future caregivers*. I am quite confident I will be wandering the halls in the middle of the night looking for my light therapy box and my old laptop so I can finish writing this book!

In particular, light therapy and melatonin—both of which I will cover later—have great results in the elderly suffering from sundown syndrome. Limiting caffeine and daytime naps also helps, as does any light exercise such as walking.

Shift Workers

Light therapy and melatonin can also help those 11 p.m.–7 a.m. workers whose circadian rhythms are off. Some people are drawn to the night shift because of their Seasonal Affective Disorder. You will learn the science behind why this is in the next chapter, but SAD is a type of circadian rhythm disorder that messes with your internal body clock. Likewise, many people who start working the night shift, in turn, notice that their new schedule affects more than just their social life. These might be people who have never been depressed a day in their life but gradually find the lack of natural light from working nights and sleeping during the day leads into depression.

My Mom the Night Nurse

A special shout-out to my Mom, who is a Registered Nurse and spent many years of her career working the challenging 11 p.m.–7 a.m. night shift with the elderly in nursing homes. She also has suffered greatly from Seasonal Affective Disorder, long before it was a recognized condition. She spent years of her life feeling truly exhausted and trying to catch up on sleep while raising us *challenging* children. *Clearly, both her and my father did an awesome job raising all three of us!* Thanks Mom and Dad! We love you!

One Billion SAD of All Ages

Now that we know there are more than 1 billion of us of all ages affected by Seasonal Affective Disorder, let's talk about "where" all these SAD people are.

Where: It's a SAD World

Seasonal Affective Disorder affects various types of people, but is more it is more common in geographic regions that are more than 30 degrees north or south of the equator. This is due to the shorter days and lack of sunlight during the winter months. Basically, the greater the distance that people are away from the earth's equator directly correlates with a higher statistical rate of SAD within the general population.

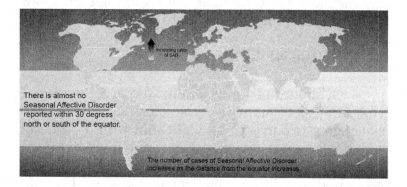

Dr. Norman Rosenthal, one of the pioneering researchers in Seasonal Affective Disorder, references several geographical studies in his book "Winter Blues." His research indicates that in the United States there is an approximate one percent prevalence of SAD in Florida. This rate increases to six percent in

Maryland and more than nine percent in New Hampshire.

Other studies suggest some anomalies in geographic location worldwide and Seasonal Affective Disorder. Interestingly, despite its Arctic location, Iceland has only a 3.8 % prevalence of SAD. There seem to be several theories about why SAD rates are lower in Iceland than in other countries at similar latitudes. These theories include the culture, diet high in fish and Omega 3s, and genetic factors.

But Why?

We have covered the Who, What, When, and Where of SAD. Time to tackle the big question with scientific explanations that will satisfy the question of every inquisitive 4-year-old. Why are we SAD?

JOZZIE RAY

Why do I have

Seasonal Affective Disorder?

It is a little tough to make this science stuff funny. I hate to admit it, but the geek in me finds this stuff pretty interesting. I tried to keep this chapter straight to the point, and hopefully somewhat interesting. Ultimately, it is important to understand what causes Seasonal Affective Disorder so that you can better understand why certain treatments work.

It's a little like the "Karate Kid" movie. Without knowing why you are doing "wax on" and "wax off," you are not motivated to keep doing it simply because you were instructed to do so. Same principle here: If you don't understand why light therapy or other treatments are working for you, are you really going to keep doing them just because someone told you to?

So try your best to pay attention young grasshopper!

Let There Be Light

During late fall and early winter, the decreased amount of sunlight causes a biochemical change in the brains of people with Seasonal Affective Disorder. It is very similar to the physiological response that causes birds to migrate and other animals to hibernate. SAD is more than just a feeling of "hating winter." There is an actual shift in brain chemicals and hormones that directly impacts a person's health and bodily functions including mood, energy, and sleep.

Some people are just genetically more sensitive to the change in light, which might explain why SAD affects certain people and leaves others unaffected. One of the main causes of winter blues is this biological reaction involving our internal body clock, or circadian rhythms, due to the shorter days and lack of sunlight. The decrease in light causes your body to increase its production of melatonin, the sleep hormone.

Sunlight is received through receptors in the eye and then travels down the optic nerve to an area of the brain called the hypothalamus. More specifically, light is processed within the hypothalamus at two groups of neurons called the suprachiasmatic nucleus (SCN). The suprachiasmatic nucleus is, in essence, the control center for our internal body clocks or circadian rhythms.

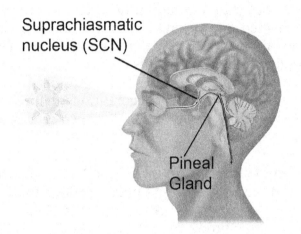

The SCN relays information to several areas of the brain, including the pineal gland, which releases melatonin, causing us to be tired or sleepy. Serotonin is needed to make melatonin, and in turn the excess melatonin production depletes serotonin levels, which negatively impacts mood.

As an off-topic side note for my hippie friends out there, the pineal gland is also thought to be the "third eye" or ajna chakra. René Descartes, dubbed the modern father of philosophy, back in the 1600s conducted research on the pineal gland. He believed it was, in essence, the point of connection between the body and intellect. The pineal gland is a small pinecone-shaped gland about the size of a piece of rice located deep in the middle of the brain.

Gene Mutation in Eye

Research pinpoints the light sensitivity of Seasonal Affective Disorder to a mutation in a gene in the eye. Light is detected and received through our eyes and sends a signal down the optic nerve to our brain. The amount of light and when light is received triggers our brains to release chemicals such serotonin and melatonin. Lack of light creates conditions that result in increased levels of melatonin and in turn decreased levels of serotonin.

A study found in the November 2008 issue of the *Journal of Affective Disorders* links a gene mutation in the eye to Seasonal Affective Disorder. The melanopsin gene produces a light-sensitive protein found in the photoreceptor of the retina of the eye. While this protein is not directly involved in vision, the protein is linked with the body's circadian rhythms and hormones that affect sleep patterns and mood.

The gene mutation affects how people respond to light and could explain why light therapy is an effective treatment. However, not all people with SAD have the gene mutation. There seem to be indicators that people with lighter-colored eyes might be more sensitive to Seasonal Affective Disorder.

Circadian Rhythms

When you suffer from Seasonal Affective Disorder, your circadian rhythms are disrupted or out of sync. Our internal "body clock" pattern is also known as our circadian rhythm. More specifically, the term circadian rhythm refers to biological patterns that cycle throughout a 24-hour period, including our sleep and wake cycle. Our circadian rhythm or body clock patterns are influenced by release of the hormones such as melatonin. These hormones, in turn, determine when we feel tired and sleepy versus when we feel awake.

Another hormone that the suprachiasmatic nucleus regulates as part of our circadian rhythm is cortisol. Cortisol is produced by the adrenal gland, which is located above the kidney. Cortisol gets a bad rap publicly as the "stress hormone." However, it is necessary to have energy. Amounts of cortisol increase in the morning, creating a sense of alertness, and decrease in the evening. Cortisol also raises blood sugar and blood pressure.

If cortisol levels are low, a person might have low blood pressure, fatigue, hypoglycemia (low blood sugar), PMS, or inability to deal with stress, among other symptoms. Cortisol levels also have an effect on how your thyroid and immune system function also. People with Seasonal Affective Disorder tend to have low levels of cortisol, especially in the morning making it difficult to wake up among other symptoms.

Circadian rhythms also adjust our body temperature, which cycles through a pattern each day. Your body temperature can vary by as much as one degree during this 24-hour cycle. Your temperature dips at night when it is time to sleep and rises slightly in the morning, indicating it is time to wake up. The drop in body temperature at night explains why people generally sleep better in bedrooms that are cool, but toss and turn on warm nights. Lower body temperature is associated with a slower metabolic rate, which is another factor in SAD.

Neurotransmitters and Hormones

The brain consists of billions of nerve cells called neurons. These brain cells communicate, or relay information to each other, by sending a chemical messenger across the synapse. The synapse is the gap or the space between each neuron, or nerve cell. The chemical messenger is called a neurotransmitter.

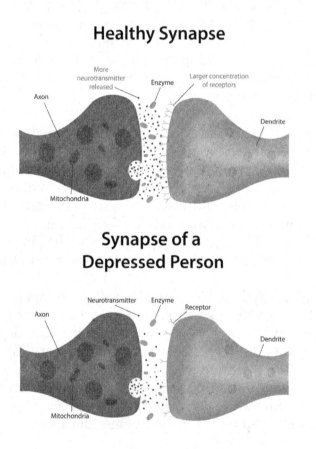

Healthy Synapse

More neurotransmitter released

Enzyme

Larger concentration of receptors

Axon

Dendrite

Mitochondria

Synapse of a Depressed Person

Neurotransmitter

Enzyme

Receptor

Axon

Dendrite

Mitochondria

The neuron releasing the brain chemicals is called the presynaptic neuron and the one receiving the neurotransmitter is called the postsynaptic neuron. The postsynaptic neuron has receptors to which the neurotransmitter binds to.

One of two scenarios can happen to the excess neurotransmitters released into the synapse. They can either be deactivated by enzymes or recycled back to the presynaptic neuron through a neurotransmitter transporter. It is referred to as re-uptake when neurotransmitters are reabsorbed back into the presynaptic neuron. People with depression generally have two abnormalities. They produce less of the necessary neurotransmitters and they also have less receptors to receive these neurotransmitters.

A recent study released in late 2014 conducted at the University of Copenhagan in Denmark discovered that levels of neurotransmitter transporters increased in patients with Seasonal Affective Disorder in the winter months. They are called serotonin transporter proteins or SERTS. *The SERTS are basically vacuuming up the serotonin out of your synapses before it can be received by the other neuron.*

When talking about Seasonal Affective Disorder and treatments, it is important to understand the following main neurotransmitters: serotonin and melatonin and also dopamine and norepinephrine.

These brain chemicals or neurotransmitters directly influence our behavior, moods, and energy levels. If these neurotransmitters are even mildly out of balance, it can cause you to feel tired, unfocused, or sluggish. If they are more severely out of balance, more severe depression, mental disorders, physical problems, or drug abuse are difficulties that might occur.

These neurotransmitters can also be considered hormones. When released in the brain to send messages, they are called neurotransmitters. However, when released as the chemical messengers of the endocrine system, they are called hormones.

Melatonin and Serotonin

Melatonin: The Sleep Hormone

Melatonin is known as the "sleep hormone" because it is the brain chemical that causes us to be tired and want to sleep. The production of melatonin is triggered by darkness, or lack of light. When the photoreceptors in the eye detect the change in light, they signal the pineal gland to begin producing melatonin. Light is like the "off switch" and causes production of melatonin to stop.

The pineal gland manufactures melatonin from another neurotransmitter called serotonin. Serotonin greatly affects your mood and emotions, and it drives your behavior. Low levels of serotonin are directly linked to depression. The majority of our serotonin is actually in our digestive tract. There is a direct link, if you will, between our brains and our "guts."

Since the days are much shorter during the winter and there is less sunlight, the body naturally produces more melatonin, thus making us tired. Likewise, the body uses more serotonin to produce the extra melatonin. There is a direct cause-and-effect relationship between melatonin and serotonin levels.

Serotonin

Low levels of serotonin can produce anxiety, negative thoughts, strong sugar cravings, excessive worrying, and sadness. In addition to mood issues, serotonin is involved in appetite, bowel movements, sleep, memory, mood, and learning. Low levels of serotonin can adversely affect these biological functions.

Lack of exercise, lack of sleep, and poorly managed stress are also known to deplete serotonin levels. Omega 3 deficiency, poor diet, and consuming too much caffeine or alcohol further deplete the levels of this important neurotransmitter.

With ideal levels of serotonin, you feel hopeful and optimistic. You are more in control of your impulses— including your appetite. Low levels of serotonin also create strong cravings for carbohydrates.

The Miracle of 5-HTP To Boost Serotonin

The amino acid tryptophan is needed to manufacture serotonin. Tryptophan is found in protein. Tryptophan is converted by the body into 5-hydroxytryptophan, or 5-HTP. Since it is a multi-step process, there can be problems that prohibit the body from converting tryptophan to 5-HTP. While tryptophan provides your body the raw material it needs to create more serotonin, 5-HTP provides your body the "ready-to-assemble" materials needed to produce more serotonin.

5-HTP provides the natural raw materials for your brain to create enough serotonin to be happy. It is available as a supplement that you can typically purchase at a vitamin store or local pharmacy. Visit **http://TheHappySun.com/Store** for a list of sources where you can purchase 5-HTP. Tryptophan is not widely available as a supplement, but 5 HTP is. 5-HTP is superior to tryptophan because it has already been converted into the most usable form to make serotonin.

5-HTP is a very effective natural treatment for winter depression. It tends to work quickly, and many people who take it often notice results within 10 days. A typical antidepressant might take six to eight weeks to become effective. Physicians might advise against taking 5-HTP if you are using a prescription antidepressant, because it might result in creating too much serotonin. Using 5-HTP in conjunction with vitamin B6 makes it more effective in creating serotonin.

The National Institutes of Health (NIH) discovered that light can be used to naturally create the mood-boosting chemical serotonin. Light therapy is now considered to be one of the most effective treatments to naturally produce serotonin, which explains why it is an effective treatment for winter depression.

Dopamine and Norepinephrine

Dopamine and norepinephrine share a similar cyclical relationship like serotonin and melatonin. Norepinephrine is manufactured from dopamine. If your dopamine levels are low, then your norepinephrine levels also most likely are low. The amino acid tryptophan is converted to 5-HTP to produce serotonin. Likewise, the amino acid tyrosine is converted to L-Dopa to create dopamine. Low levels of dopamine and, in turn, norepinephrine, have also been noted in people with SAD.

Dopamine

Dopamine is a neurotransmitter that helps control the brain's pleasure centers. It is also involved in motor coordination and regulating emotional responses.

Dopamine also affects circadian rhythms, specifically involving body heat production and heat loss via the vascular system. Dopamine levels influence motivation, interest, and drive. Dopamine levels also affect appetite.

High levels of dopamine can lead to aggressive behaviors, and low levels tend to cause slowed reactions. People with low dopamine activity are also more prone to ADHD and addiction issues. Parkinson's disease is linked with dopamine deficiency, due to the loss of dopamine-producing neurons. In addition to treating SAD, new studies are showing promising results for light therapy as being an effective treatment for Parkison's Disease as well.

Norepinephrine

Low levels of norepinephrine can result in lethargy, decreased energy, and decreased mental alertness. Norepinephrine is also involved in mood, pain, and cognition and—together with epinephrine—is responsible for the fight-or-flight response.

Amino Acid Tyrosine

Your body makes dopamine from the amino acid tyrosine. Tyrosine is also needed to manufacture norepinephrine. Enzymes convert tyrosine into L-Dopa and another enzyme then converts L-Dopa into dopamine. An additional enzyme and chemical reaction is needed to convert the dopamine into norepinephrine.

Tyrosine is found in food such as bananas, almonds, pumpkin seeds, low-fat dairy, meats, and poultry. You can also purchase L-Tyrosine as a supplement. Mucuna pruriens is a bean that grows in the tropics. It is very rich in natural L-Dopa. Either L Tyrosine or Dopa Mucuna is available as a supplement. Visit **http://TheHappySun.com/Store** for more details on where to purchase.

Light therapy can also increase dopamine levels. Light signals receptors in the retina of the eye to release dopamine. Supplementing with both 5-HTP and Dopa Mucuna can be a winning combination in helping to combat Seasonal Affective Disorder.

STOP! MUST READ! Summary or Short Version of This Chapter

If you dozed off during this chapter or found your brain wandering to more interesting thoughts, let me try to summarize some key points. Try to wake up and pay attention to this summary now, or I will have to send a nun to your house to hit your knuckles with a ruler!

There is a good chance that you have a genetic mutation in the receptor of your eye that makes you more sensitive to light. Your eye receives the light, and it travels down your optic nerve to an area of your brain that controls your sleep-wake cycles, or circadian rhythms. The amount of light tells your body how much melatonin or sleep hormone your body should release. Your body uses serotonin, which is your good mood brain chemical, to create melatonin.

The lack of light causes the body to start pumping excess melatonin, making you feel sleepy. Light acts as the "off switch" signaling your body to stop producing melatonin. Since it is dark out your brain thinks you should be sleeping. To manufacture all this sleepy melatonin, your brain is also zapping up the supply of all your "good mood" brain chemical, serotonin. The low levels of serotonin have a huge effect on your mood and appetite.

The lack of light also affects our internal body clocks, or circadian rhythms, and has an impact on cortisol production. Cortisol is made by the adrenal glands, and low levels of cortisol make it difficult for a person to have the energy they need to wake up and get moving in the morning. Circadian rhythms affect our sleep wake cycle and also have an effect on body temperature and metabolism.

You may not be receiving enough of key brain chemicals called neurotransmitters. Important neurotransmitters for Seasonal Affective Disorder include serotonin, dopamine and norepinephrine. Additionally, there are most likely less receptors on your brain cells called neurons to receive these important chemicals.

Your body is trying to get more serotonin and starts triggering strong cravings for carbohydrates in an attempt to self-medicate. 5-HTP is made from the amino acid tryptophan. Taking 5-HTP as a supplement can help your body create more serotonin naturally and is an effective treatment to combat

Seasonal Affective Disorder, especially when combined with light therapy.

In addition, another brain chemical or neurotransmitter called dopamine has been found to be low in people with Seasonal Affective Disorder. Dopamine is needed to create another brain chemical, norepinephrine, which effects your energy levels. L-Tyrosine is the amino acid that is converted to L-Dopa to then create dopamine, and in turn norepinephrine. Both L-Tyrosine and Dopa Mucuna are available as supplements. Taking one or the other may help raise dopamine levels.

Most prescription antidepressants are attempting to alter a combination of serotonin, dopamine, or norepinephrine levels. Antidepressants create a synthetic reaction and can also cause uncomfortable side effects. 5-HTP and L-Tyrosine are natural amino acids and effective treatments for Seasonal Affective Disorder as well as other forms of depression. These supplements provide your body with the raw materials it needs to naturally build and increase your levels of serotonin, dopamine, and norepinephrine.

Low levels of dopamine are noted in those with ADHD and addiction issues. Low levels of dopamine are also probably part of the reason why you might have had difficulty paying attention to this chapter ... and why I had problems writing it.

Summary

To summarize there are several biological reactions resulting in the root causes of SAD:

- Lack of light results in excess melatonin production (sleep hormone)
- Serotonin levels decrease as it needed to make melatonin
- Less receptors on your brain cells (neurons) to receive serotonin
- Higher levels of neurotransmitter transporters (SERT) immediately reabsorbing serotonin
- Low cortisol levels (making it difficult to wake up)
- Circadian rhythm issues (sleep wake cycle, low body temperature & reduced metabolism)
- Low dopamine levels (motivation, interest & drive)
- Low norepinephrine levels (lethargy & energy)

If you still had trouble with all this science stuff, I can help you by summarizing this chapter in once sentence.

Being left in the dark too long makes your brain SAD!

Naturally SAD

Environmental Factors

If you read the previous chapter, or at least the summary, you will hopefully understand that Seasonal Affective Disorder is a biological response to how your body processes light. Your brain chemicals actually increase and decrease based on the amount of light, causing your symptoms. The change in light also has a strong effect on plants, animals, and our natural environment. It triggers biological responses such as hibernation, migration, and photosynthesis. Unfortunately, for humans, it is apparently socially unacceptable to hibernate for the winter.

Weather

The weather has an impact on people suffering from Seasonal Affective Disorder. SAD sufferers are generally more sensitive to the cold since their metabolic rates slow down, in essence our bodies are trying to prepare for human hibernation. (My husband will solemnly swear that during the winter my hands and feet are colder than those of a dead person.) The temperature, barometric pressure, and humidity can also factor into the equation.

Rainy Days in the Summer

However, Seasonal Affective Disorder is caused primarily by the diminishing amounts, or absence, of sunlight. Several consecutive rainy or cloudy days in a row can trigger depressive symptoms even in the middle of summer. For me, usually by the third or fourth rainy day in a row, I notice a shift in my mood and attitude.

Hibernation and Migration

Hmm, does all this science remind you of anything? Let me refresh your memory about a couple things you learned in grade school science class called migration and hibernation. Migration and hibernation patterns occur over the course of a year and are referred to as circannual rhythms.

The definition of hibernation is basically an inactive state resembling a deep sleep in which certain animals living in cold climates pass the winter. Body temperature is lowered, and breathing and heart rates slow down. Hibernation is a survival mechanism that protects an animal from the cold and reduces the need for food during the season when it is scarce.

Birds can also sense the decrease in light, and this decrease in light is a trigger that causes them to migrate. Recent research confirms that birds also have a light-sensitive pineal gland. Just like in us humans, the lack of light also causes increases in the level of melatonin in their little bird brains directly resulting in their desire to migrate.

Random Author's Comment:

Perhaps that is a better way to describe Seasonal Affective Disorder. We all have bird brains. Who knows, maybe flying south for the winter to get more light is really just the bird version of light therapy.

Why the Leaves Change Color

Our individual light sensitivity is similar to why some plants require full sun while others thrive in the shade. This is a simplistic way of understanding why SAD affects some people while others feel perfectly fine during the fall and winter.

The decrease in daylight during the autumn months also triggers leaves to change color. During the spring and summer, chlorophyll in plant cells absorbs the sun's light energy and uses it for photosynthesis. Photosynthesis is the chemical reaction process in which light energy is used to transform carbon dioxide and water into sugars, or basically "tree food." These sugars, or tree food, are actually carbohydrates.

This process of photosynthesis gradually slows in the fall, stopping the production of chlorophyll. Without chlorophyll leaves lose their green color. The bright color of their underlying pigment is revealed. Temperature and moisture also factor in how vibrantly the leaves change color because these variables affect how much sugar is produced in the leaves. Warm, sunny days and cool (but not freezing) nights result in the most brilliant color displays.

Photosynthesis cannot occur without chlorophyll, and the leaves no longer create sugar. The leaves actually transfer the sugar to roots, branches, and trunk to save so that the tree has food stored to be used to get through winter and be available for spring growth.

Random Author's Comment:

Bottom line is that, basically, even trees are load up on carbohydrates for the winter. This gives a whole new meaning to the phrase having "junk in the trunk!"

Why Squirrels Gather Nuts

The decrease in sunlight also affects a squirrel's pineal gland and, in turn, causes an increase of levels of melatonin. This increase in levels of melatonin triggers their food-hoarding behavior, causing them to scurry around gathering nuts for the winter. The increased melatonin might also cause squirrels to sleep longer hours and thickens their fur, preparing them for the colder winter.

Certain breeds of squirrels store their nuts in multiple locations and then actually forget where they buried them. These squirrels are trying to protect their stash by diversifying, but since they forget where they buried them, they inadvertently actually end up planting trees. *It seems that these squirrels might also seem to be suffering from a little ADHD as well!*

Since Humans Shouldn't Hibernate

I hate when I get suckered in by a catchy title on the cover of a magazine, only to struggle to figure out which article it references and what page it is on. Then I read the article and still cannot find a direct answer to the intriguing title I was enticed with. In an effort to have some literary integrity, here is the part referenced in the title of this book "Since Humans Shouldn't Hibernate."

The change in light affects our brain chemicals and triggers very primal biological responses. It is very similar to what causes birds to migrate south and other animals to hibernate for the winter. It also causes the leaves to change color on certain types of trees. Some plants need full sun to survive, while others thrive in the shade. Some humans adapt well to winter, but those of us with Seasonal Affective Disorder do best in full sun.

Unfortunately, society dictates that it is simply not practical for humans to quit their jobs and hibernate for the winter, despite our overwhelming biological urge to do so. Nor does it seem realistic for most of us humans to migrate north and south with the seasons like birds do ... unless we are retired.

The humans who don't have Seasonal Affective Disorder may not understand our winter dilemma and expect us to be awake and productive all year long. *"Since humans shouldn't hibernate,"* let's discuss some treatment options for sufferers of Seasonal Affective Disorder so we can at least function with the other humans during the winter. Before we do, I want to discuss other conditions that may be related to SAD.

Other Conditions Related to

Seasonal Affective Disorder

As you learned in the previous chapters, the imbalance in brain chemicals or neurotransmitters results in the depressive symptoms associated with Seasonal Affective Disorder. This same imbalance in brain chemicals is also linked with other medical conditions. It is not uncommon to have Seasonal Affective Disorder and ADHD, because both are caused by an imbalance in dopamine levels as well as levels of other neurotransmitters.

People with SAD are also known to have some of the following related medical conditions:

- Bipolar Disorder
- Attention Deficit Hyperactivity Disorder (ADHD)
- Thyroid Issues
- Alcohol and Addiction Issues
- Sleep Issues or Insomnia
- Chronic Fatigue Syndrome

- Fibromyalgia
- Weight Issues

The root causes of many of these issues also have to do with imbalances in brain chemistry. Some of the treatments for Seasonal Affective Disorder might help alleviate issues associated with these other related medical conditions.

Reverse Seasonal Affective Disorder

Summer SAD

This book is geared toward the more "popular and traditional" winter depression, since that is what the author suffers from. If you have "Reverse Seasonal Affective Disorder," or Summer Depression, you might have to read this book somewhat like a dyslexic person and just reverse the information.

While those of us with winter depression are busy frolicking about during the summer months, there are some people who suffer from a seasonal pattern of depression that strikes when the weather's warm. This summer depression often tends to bring about more symptoms of anxiety and irritability. Other symptoms of this type of reverse Seasonal Affective Disorder include trouble sleeping in the summer months and an overall sense of agitation.

Summer Depression Symptoms

The symptoms exhibited during the summer months might include the following:

- Anxiety
- Insomnia
- Irritability
- Agitation

Other physical symptoms of Summer SAD can include headaches and weight loss.

What Causes Summer SAD?

It has been theorized that the hot weather and humidity might be to blame for reverse Seasonal Affective Disorder. While some researchers suggest that the high temperatures might play a role, others suggest that allergies might play a role. According to George Shannon, MD, a family practitioner in Columbus, Ga., reverse Seasonal Affective Disorder is actually thought to be a form of bipolar disorder.

However, if you re-read the chapter "What Causes Winter Depression" you can see how this same information might be reversed and applied toward those with Summer SAD. While people with Winter Depression are lacking in serotonin due to how their eyes process light, people with Summer Depression might in fact be creating too much serotonin during the summer months. Summer SAD symptoms might be very similar to what is known as Serotonin Syndrome.

Taking melatonin supplements during the summer months has been shown to be very helpful to some people suffering from Reverse Seasonal Affective Disorder. Melatonin helps reduce the abundance of serotonin that the excess light is creating, causing their irritability and other SAD symptoms. Melatonin has proved effective for treating Summer SAD in the same manner that 5-HTP has proved to help boost the serotonin of those suffering from winter depression. Unfortunately, this information is not widely known. Gaba is another amino acid supplement that might assist in helping to relax people or calm their anxiety.

Bipolar Disorder

Bipolar is a mood disorder characterized by the cycling between depression and hypomania. There are several different subtypes of this disorder listed in the DSM, depending upon how frequently and in what manner the symptoms appear. Alternating between two opposing states of highs and lows is in essence the definition of bipolar. These extreme mood swings can result in major disruptions to a person's quality of life.

The depressive symptoms can include sadness, loss of energy, trouble concentrating, an increase in appetite, weight gain, and lethargy. Often, the person experiences feelings of hopelessness or feels worthless. This depressive state is considered "the lows" of Bipolar. These symptoms are very similar to those seen in Major Depressive Disorder. The difference between Bipolar Disorder and Depression is the shift to a manic state or mood.

During a manic state, people with Bipolar Disorder are experiencing "the highs" of Bipolar. They often exhibit symptoms that include excessive happiness, feelings of grandiosity, rapid speech pattern, impulsiveness, and often irritability. There is usually a reduced need for sleep and an increase in sex drive. During this manic phase, a person often makes impulsive and sometimes dangerous decisions.

Studies show that many people with Bipolar might also have ADHD. There is also a link between both conditions and substance abuse issues. There is some discussion in medical communities about whether Seasonal Affective Disorder is a variant of Bipolar Disorder. Technically, according the "Diagnostic and Statistical Manual of Mental Disorders (DSM)," Bipolar Disorder has its own diagnostic criteria, while SAD is a "specifier" of depression. The DSM continues to evolve and change as medical studies uncover new information.

There are studies that prove links between Bipolar Disorder and Seasonal Affective Disorder. Both disorders are clearly caused by a similar chemical imbalance in the brain, as was discussed in the previous chapter. Many of the same treatments, including light therapy, help depressive symptoms in both conditions.

Attention Deficit Hyperactivity Disorder (ADHD)

Research conducted at the University of Rochester links Seasonal Affective Disorder (SAD) to Attention Deficit Hyperactivity Disorder (ADHD) and alcoholism.

Other researchers from the American College of Neuropsychopharmacology have been also studying how dopamine plays a role in Seasonal Affective Disorder. A study published in 2004 indicates that there is sufficient evidence that people with Seasonal Affective Disorder experience altered dopamine activity. In particular, the dopamine receptor 4 gene plays a role in Attention Deficit Disorder (ADD) and body weight regulation.

The depression symptoms of SAD and inattention symptoms of ADHD can often overlap. Since the onset of Seasonal Affective Disorder is usually in late fall or early winter, SAD coincides with the school year calendar. Thus, it is often a teacher who notices problems in a child that these conditions affect.

While ADHD has received widespread attention in recent years, SAD, often known as "Winter Depression," is often undiagnosed or overlooked in physician's offices, especially in children.

Winter depression can make it difficult for a child to concentrate in class. They might also be experiencing sleep disturbances or night wakings, which, in turn, exasperate the problem. The lethargy usually leads to a decreased interest in activity. Often, a child loses interest and drops out of a favorite sport or activity he or she enjoys.

Children and adults with SAD will often try to "self-medicate" with food. Cravings for sweets and carbohydrates are very pronounced. Alcoholism can be a common problem for adults.

Similarly, spring and summer can often bring about "mania" or hyperactivity in people with Seasonal Affective Disorder. It is understandable how SAD symptoms can often be assumed to be ADHD.

Treatment options are available for children with ADHD and SAD. Light therapy can be an extremely effective way to treat these children. A high-protein diet limiting highly processed foods with chemical additives can also make a difference. Medication is a personal decision to be discussed with a qualified physician.

Supplementing with the amino acid L-Tyrosine or Dopa Mucuna might help increase dopamine levels naturally. New and engaging activities and hobbies also help raise dopamine levels. Exercise is also an important factor.

There is a book, that I consider a must read for anyone with ADHD. It is written by Dr. Daniel Amen and is called "Healing ADD: The Breakthrough Program that Allows You to See and Heal the 7 Types of ADD." You can also find it among other referenced resources at http://TheHappySun.com/Store.

Thyroid Issues

Your thyroid is a gland located in the front of your neck that produces thyroid hormone. Thyroid hormone controls the way the body uses energy. If your body produces too much of this hormone, the resulting condition is called hyperthyroidism. If your body produces too little of the thyroid hormone, the resulting condition is called hypothyroidism, which is also referred to as an underactive thyroid.

Having an underactive thyroid or hypothyroidism is linked to depression and SAD. Since the thyroid affects how the body uses energy, a lower body temperature is a common symptom, which might explain why certain people do not tolerate the cold. Other symptoms of an underactive thyroid include the following:

- Exhaustion and Fatigue
- Weight Gain
- Brittle Fingernails
- Constipation
- Dry Skin
- Intolerance or Sensitivity to the Cold
- Cold Hands and Feet
- Slowed Heart Rate
- Muscle Aches and Stiffness

There are other symptoms, as well, which range from infertility issues to thin eyebrows that can be affected by hypothyroidism.

Diagnosing thyroid problems can be a challenge, because traditional lab results often show "normal thyroid" levels despite a long list of patient symptoms that can indicate a thyroid issue. Blood tests measure levels of Thyroid Stimulating Hormone (TSH). T3 and T4 levels should be tested as part of that blood test. Over the past several years, there has been some change in what is considered normal range or normal levels.

Dr. Broda Barnes was an American physician who studied the endocrine system and published several medical books, and one in particular on hypothyroidism. He promoted a diagnostic test that can be done at home to test for underactive thyroid, which is known as the "Barnes Basal Temperature Test."

The Barnes Basal Temperature Test suggests taking your temperature before you get out of bed each morning. The reading should be recorded immediately upon awakening before getting out of bed or engaging in any activity. Typically, a basal body temperature below 97.8 degrees is thought to indicate hypothyroidism.

A woman's menstrual cycle can affect her basal temperature, so as a general guideline it is best to start testing around the second day of your period. This is because the body temperature tends to rise during ovulation.

For years I suspected that I had an underactive thyroid, but my blood work always came back in the normal range. I exhibited most of the symptoms listed above. (My husband will testify that both my hands and feet are colder than a dead person's especially in the winter!) After reading about the Barnes basal temperature test, I decided to try it. For several weeks, I took body temperature upon waking up before getting out of bed and it was consistently low.

After reviewing the results and further discussion of my symptoms, my physician started me on a trial of Amour thyroid medication. Within one week of starting a trial, I called my physician crying and thanking her. The dense brain fog and complete exhaustion was lifting, and felt better than I had in years. Having an under active thyroid in addition to Seasonal Affective Disorder is a very depressing combination of symptoms. I continue to take Amour thyroid to this day, and my blood work still shows "normal" levels.

Amour thyroid medication is actually derived from the glands of pigs. This particular medication has been around since the 1900s, and it contains T3 and T4 as well as other thyroid hormones. It is thought to be more natural than the traditional synthetic drugs that pharmaceutical companies manufacture such as Synthroid or Levothroid, as many contain only T4 and not T3.

Pharmaceutical companies do not profit from Amour thyroid medication and push for physicians to prescribe the companies' newer synthetic drugs. As a side note, there was sudden shortage of Amour thyroid a few years ago. This caused many people to switch to the more readily available brands such as Synthroid or Levothroid. I was able to have a compounding lab continue to make my medication. However it had to be shipped via mail order and I paid out of pocket during this shortage.

Alcohol and Addiction Issues

Using alcohol or drugs to try and self-medicate is very common for people with SAD. The decreased amount of sunlight creates a biochemical change in the brains of people with this disorder. In essence, the person is trying to correct the underlying chemical imbalances in his or her brain by taking these substances to feel better.

These behaviors do provide a slight chemical boost, which is why it is difficult to break these habits even though they are not healthy behaviors. For example, cigarettes, affect the neurotransmitter dopamine, stimulating the brain's pleasure center. If you are feeling depressed due to a chemical imbalance, it only makes sense that you would be drawn to a something that increases that brain chemical even if it is an unhealthy behavior. Depression and alcoholism often go hand in hand. When a person is depressed, he or she has low levels of serotonin in the brain. Serotonin affects both mood and impulse control.

Unfortunately, this type of behavior is cyclical. The food or substance is not actually fixing the underlying biochemical imbalance, but is instead creating a series of highs and lows. It is the equivalent of being on a roller coaster. Impulse control is low because of the decreased serotonin, and it is difficult to stop the cycle.

Other Resources for Further Information

There are several books that discuss the chemical imbalances in the brain and addiction issues in more detail. It is very common for people who struggle with drugs and alcohol to suffer from nutritional deficiencies. Specifically Niacin, or Vitamin B3 can be very helpful in this area.

Seven Weeks to Sobriety by Joan Mathews Larson, Ph.D.

"Seven Weeks to Sobriety" is dedicated to exploring the nutritional deficiency in those battling with alcohol. It gets to the root cause of the problem and helps in truly healing the body. Specific treatment strategies are depending upon answers to detailed questionnaires in the book. If you or a loved one has struggled with this issue, this is a must-read book in helping to stop the vicious cycle.

Unchain Your Brain by Daniel Amen, M.D and David E. Smith, M.D.

"Unchain Your Brain" is another important must read book for those struggling with addiction issues. Different types of drugs affect different areas of the brain. The imbalance of brain chemicals or neurotransmitters in certain areas of the brain result cravings for certain types of drugs. Detailed strategies are discussed depending upon which drug of choice a person is drawn toward.

Both of these books can be found online at The Happy Sun store or **http://TheHappySun.com/store.**

Chronic Fatigue Syndrome and Fibromyalgia

The symptom list for Chronic Fatigue Syndrome (CFS), Fibromyalgia, and depression are very similar. They can overlap, and it can be difficult to clearly distinguish one from another. Sometimes, if these symptoms appear and diminish on a seasonal cycle, they can be related to Seasonal Affective Disorder.

Other times, such symptoms might be experienced year round and further complicate the health and well-being of people with SAD. Some of the SAD treatments can help to alleviate some of the symptoms of Fibromyalgia and CFS by raising serotonin levels.

Chronic Fatigue Syndrome (CFS) Symptoms

- Extreme exhaustion and sickness following physical activity or mental exertion
- Problems with sleep
- Difficulties with memory and concentration
- Persistent muscle pain
- Joint pain (without redness or swelling)
- Headache
- Tender lymph nodes in the neck or armpit
- Sore throat
- Brain fog
- Difficulty maintaining an upright position, dizziness, balance problems, or fainting
- Allergies or sensitivities to foods, odors, chemicals, medications, or noise
- Irritable bowels
- Chills and night sweats
- Visual disturbances (sensitivity to light, blurring, eye pain)
- Depression or mood problems (irritability, mood swings, anxiety, panic attacks)

Fibromyalgia Symptoms

- Deep muscle pain and soreness
- Morning stiffness
- Flu-like aching
- Radiating pain
- Sensitivity to touch

- Problems sleeping
- Fatigue
- Difficulty thinking clearly, also known as "fibro fog"
- Difficulty performing everyday tasks
- Stress and anxiety
- Depression
- Migraine headaches
-

Weight Issues

Simply put, depression makes you tired! It is hard to exercise when it is cold and dark outside and all you want to do is sit on the couch or sleep. New Year's resolutions never last long, because we are starting them in the middle of our winter funk. Our best intentions quickly fall off track because our cravings for food are essentially a form of self-medication. Unfortunately, the result is often unwanted weight gain, which, in turn, makes us feel even more discouraged. Having Seasonal Affective Disorder often feels like your metabolism shuts down and you store fat like a bear for the winter.

Our behaviors often unconsciously drive us toward trying to fix the deficits in our bodies, which is why we might be repeatedly drawn to alcohol, caffeine, or carbohydrates. So while it might be our best intention to shed 15 pounds or to cut back on alcohol consumption, our cravings can be so powerful that they hinder our progress. Correcting some of these nutritional deficiencies and brain chemistry imbalances with supplements and other treatments can help you regain control of your life.

Now that we have covered a pretty depressing list of other medical issues possibly related to Seasonal Affective Disorder, let's discuss treatment options.

Adventures in Light Therapy

"Maybe we don't really have Seasonal Affective Disorder after all...

Maybe we are all just afraid of the dark."

~Jozzie Ray

Go toward the light!

We sound like a bunch of moths. It's true. We do. Whenever I read articles about Seasonal Affective Disorder treatments—and they describe light therapy—that is honestly what I think. The rest of the world thinks we are a bunch of moths clamoring in front of our lights and crying because it is winter.

Light Therapy Helps ... If You Use It

Light therapy is an extremely effective treatment for Seasonal Affective Disorder. Also known as phototherapy, light therapy involves sitting in front of a specialized light called a "light box." It can be helpful to those with even just a mild case of the winter blues. Light therapy devices use visible light and generally filter out the ultraviolet light. They will not cause you to become tan.

Light therapy has been widely studied and proven to help SAD sufferers. In the chapter, "Why Do I Have Seasonal Affective Disorder," I discuss in detail how the body processes light to produce serotonin and melatonin and regulates circadian rhythms.

Understanding the science behind those processes helps explain why light therapy is effective. Light therapy is also known to be helpful in treating other conditions such as depression, Bipolar Depression, PMS, Bulimia Nervosa, Chronic Fatigue Syndrome, jet lag and insomnia.

How and When to Use Light Therapy

For most people, effective SAD treatment involves using the light box for approximately 30 minutes per day. It is generally better to use light therapy in the morning, ideally within one hour of waking up. While it might not always possible to administer treatment at those times or for the full 30 minutes, try to use light therapy daily.

There are very few reported side effects for light therapy, which makes it the preferred method of treatment. If light therapy is administered a few hours before bed, some people report insomnia, thus it is better to use the treatment in the morning. Users report seeing positive results in as little as three to five days of beginning light therapy, whereas medications can take up to six to eight weeks to work.

What Kind of Light Box Should I Buy?

For this natural remedy to be successful, it is important to be consistent with light therapy treatment. If treatment is skipped or stopped, the symptoms of Seasonal Affective Disorder can begin to reassert themselves within a few days. It is important to find a light box that will work with your lifestyle.

10,000 LUX Light Box

It is recommended that the light box be 10,000 LUX. Neither conventional nor full-spectrum light bulbs are strong enough to be effective for therapeutic treatment, though such light might enhance the overall living environment of a person suffering with SAD. Because light therapy has become known as an effective treatment, there is now a large variety of different light box styles and manufacturers.

Traditional Light Boxes

When I got my first light box back in the mid-1990s, it was a rather large square rectangle that lit up the room with the intensity of a mild nuclear explosion. It was winter in New England, but I know my neighbors were wondering what was causing the room to glow under the drawn shades. Today, thankfully, we have a few more styles and options from which to choose. We now have smaller and more portable light therapy devices. There are models designed to look like desk lamps or floor lamps.

Dawn Simulators

Another type of light therapy is the use of a "dawn simulator." A dawn simulator is essentially an alarm clock programmed to begin gradually filling the room full of light. The gradual brightening of the bedroom is meant to be similar to a natural sunrise shining through your window on a sunny summer morning.

Light therapy is an excellent solution to beginning a dark cold bleak winter day.

Find a Light Box that Fits Your Lifestyle

For light therapy to effectively lift your spirits, it is important to try and use it consistently. For most people this means being in front of your light box for 30 minutes per day, preferably in the morning. The key is to find a way to make it fit into your lifestyle. Ideally, you might have multiple light therapy devices. Perhaps you wake with a dawn simulator and then use a desk lamp device at the office.

Visit <u>http://TheHappySun.com/Store</u> for more information light therapy devices and pricing.

Tips for Living with Light Therapy

We tend to live busy and hectic lives and time for light therapy is not always possible. When too many days pass without using light therapy, symptoms of depression tend to reoccur. When you stop light therapy, you have essentially discontinued your medication. You deserve to stop and take care of yourself!

The following are some suggestions to help you try and squeeze some light into your life:

Exercise with Light

Try setting up your light box in front of a treadmill or next to the television while doing an exercise program. Exercise has also proved to enhance mood and help depression!

Computer Tips

Set up your light box on the side of your computer screen. Get light therapy while you are checking your email, surfing the web, or working.

Stuck in a cube all day? Try a light therapy box that looks like a desk lamp!

Pay your bills, read a book, or catch up on your hobbies in front of your light.

Dawn Simulators and Light Visors

Mornings just too busy to sit still? Try the dawn simulator, which works like an alarm clock. It is a light box that gradually lightens your bedroom while you sleep, simulating a nice sunrise.

You might look a little silly, but they even make light visors, which is basically a hat with light built into the visor. It is designed so you can receive light therapy, and not have to be stationary in one spot. I am not sure I can personally pull off the look, but it can be an effective way of getting in some much-needed light therapy while you are on the move.

Tips for Kids

Try a dawn simulator alarm clock to wake them up for school.

Set up the light box in front of the computer, and let them play or learn on an educational website.

Have them use the light box while doing homework.

Try doing light therapy while they draw or paint.

Put the light box on a TV tray while they indulge in their favorite television show.

Have them walk on a treadmill and set the light box next to it.

Caution about Tanning

In the winter, I crave the sun and warmth. I need to admit that in years past I have used indoor tanning beds. I paid extra for the ones that were supposed to filter out more of the ultraviolet rays. I liked tanning. It made me feel good. I thought I was being reasonable about it. I didn't go for the full amount of time or more than a couple times a week. I only went during in the winter, and there were only a handful of years that I used indoor tanning beds.

Recently, I noticed a very small freckle on my chest. The borders of it were irregular. I showed my physician, who referred me to a dermatologist. They performed a biopsy and informed me the biopsy showed abnormal cells. It was not cancer but if left untreated could it evolve into cancer.

They needed to cut more of it out. They cut out a chunk of flesh about the size of the tip of my finger. I had eight stitches. I went back for a full-body screening and had two other freckles cut out of my skin, one of which also had abnormal cells. This was not a very pleasant experience, but I am grateful it was caught early.

A former classmate and friend of mine recently passed away of melanoma. She was only 36. She left behind two young children. If it weren't for her loss, I might not have thought twice about my new small freckle. I miss you, friend. You saved my life.

I now go twice a year for full-body screenings. I no longer use an indoor tanning bed. I make sure my family uses sunscreen. Please don't use indoor tanning beds or booths. They are not safe. According to the Skin Cancer Foundation: "Based on 7 worldwide studies, people who first use a tanning bed before age 35 increase their risk for melanoma by 75 percent." If you have used a tanning bed, please schedule a full-body screening to check for skin cancer.

Visit The Skin Cancer Foundation at http://skincancer.org for more detailed information and learn your ABCDEs of melanoma.

NORMAL		CANCEROUS
	"A" IS FOR ASYMMETRY • If you draw a line through the middle of the mole, the halves of a melanoma won't match in size.	
	"B" IS FOR BORDER • The edges of an early melanoma tend to be uneven, crusty or notched.	
	"C" IS FOR COLOR • Healthy moles are uniform in color. A variety of colors, especially white and/or blue, is bad.	
	"D" IS FOR DIAMETER • Melanomas are usually larger in diameter than a pencil eraser, although they can be smaller.	
	"E" IS FOR EVOLVING • When a mole changes in size, shape or color, or begins to bleed or scab, this points to danger.	

Ear Light Therapy

There is promising new hope on the horizon if you are not a fan of sitting in front of a light box. Several studies have been conducted in Finland to test light therapy via the ear canal. In conducting research on the circadian rhythms of birds, biologist Juuso Nissila discovered light-sensitive protein on the surface of the brain.

Instead of administering light therapy via the receptors in the eyes, research was conducted to measure the effectiveness of sending light therapy via the ear canal directly to the brain. The results have been very promising. The light therapy administered via the ear canal seems to be resulting in regulation of serotonin, melatonin, and dopamine in a manner similar to traditional light box therapy received via the eye.

The ear light therapy device looks similar to a MP3 player, with ear buds that administer light into the ear canal. The company that manufactures the device, Valkee, recommends using it for 12 minutes per day. Their studies report that about 70% of the patients with Seasonal Affective Disorder experienced full remission within four weeks of use.

Negative Ion Therapy

Think about the taking a walk on the beach for a moment and breathing in the fresh air. That fresh ocean air is actually charged with negative ions. The collision of the moving air and water of the surf causes the molecules to break apart. The water molecules lose an electron and the air molecules gain one. This results in the air becoming negatively charged and the water becoming positively charged.

The air is negatively charged near waterfalls and after thunderstorms too. Forests are also full of negative ions, because all plants give off some ions. The air in both office buildings and homes are not typically negatively charged, however, because the metal in central air and heating units actually strips the negative ions, as do the synthetics used in carpets and drapes.

When the air is negatively charged the extra electron in each air molecule magnetically attracts dust and other particles. When the electron attaches to the dust or particle, it becomes heavy and fall to the ground essentially cleaning the air. Normal cleaning activities such as vacuuming or dusting then remove the particles. However without the extra electron the dust and particles continue to float and pollute the air allowing us to breathe them in.

Several studies have been conducted on the effects of negative ions and their health benefits. In particular a study that Dr. Michael Terman and Dr. Jiuan Su Terman conducted at Columbia University has shown that a high density of negative ions can be effective as part of a treatment plan for Seasonal Affective Disorder.

There are a few light boxes that also have a negative ion feature. If you suffer from allergies, you can also find some air filtration systems that offer negative ion therapy too. If you live near the ocean, try to take a drive down to the coast, and get some fresh air whenever possible. Consider it therapy for yourself.

Where to Buy

Visit **http://TheHappySun.com/Store** for information, reviews and pricing on different light therapy devices.

Vitamins, Supplements and Prescriptions

I have read over the years an awful lot about vitamins, amino acids, and holistic cures. There seems to be a miracle cure for every ailment out there. I have spent a considerable amount of money trying many of these supplements and remedies. Some helped. Some did not.

I hate to write about too many options or in too much detail regarding them because it can become overwhelming. Once something feels too overwhelming or too complicated (or too expensive), we often ditch the idea completely and won't take any supplements. I am going to explain in detail some of the important vitamins and supplements so you understand their job or function in helping you with Seasonal Affective Disorder.

The Toolbox Approach

Try to think of this chapter as a toolbox. You might not need all these tools (or supplements) every day. More often than not, you will at least need your basic tools (or vitamins). Then there will be days or weeks when a more specific set of tools will prove to be very helpful for a certain problem, but then you might not need them again for a while.

Too often we set out with the mindset that we are going to follow a plan or diet with a strict regimen. This "black and white" or "all or nothing" attitude often sets us up for failure, and we usually end up quitting the plan completely. My goal is to give you options or tools to use as needed.

Vitamin D—The Sunshine Vitamin

Vitamin D deficiency is directly linked to SAD. Chances are that if you think you might have Seasonal Affective Disorder then you are most likely vitamin D deficient. Vitamin D production decreases with age and can be hindered with the application of sunscreen. Your physician can perform blood work to test whether you are deficient.

Vitamin D has a good reputation. It is known as "the sunshine vitamin." However, some of the information I have read makes it seem like the sun magically teleports vitamin D directly into your skin. That is not exactly what happens scientifically.

Long Answer

The long answer is that the food we eat is actually oxidized and converted into a compound called 7-dehydrocholesterol or pro-vitamin D3. This compound is then transported to the epidermal layer of the skin, where it is stored inactively. The ultraviolet B rays of the sun actually trigger a chemical reaction and convert it into D3. Vitamin D3 is then sent to the liver for a second chemical reaction in which it is converted into 25-hydroxyvitamin D. Vitamin D3 is then sent to the kidneys for a third conversion by adding oxygen molecules into 1,25 dihydroxyvitamin D, or calcitriol.

Short Answer

The short answer is that your body manufactures vitamin D through the conversion of the cholesterol stored in your skin. Think of the sun as an oven that is heating up your food. The sun essentially "cooks" the cholesterol in your skin, converting it into vitamin D3 so that your body can use it. You don't want to "burn your food" by being in the sun for too long, but rather just warm it up so it is consumable. If you have darker skin, you have more melanin and will need more sun exposure to produce vitamin D.

How much vitamin D do you need?

Most physicians recommend getting between 1,000 and 2,000 IUs of vitamin D every day. Vitamin D is a fat-soluble vitamin, which means the body best absorbs the vitamin when you take it with a fat. Magnesium is a cofactor and helps the body absorb more vitamin D.

If you are taking a weight loss aid that is designed to block fat, this aid will also prevent your body from absorbing vitamin D. Antacids and other medications can also interfere with vitamin D absorption.

Fish and egg yolks have vitamin D in notable quantities. Milk is usually fortified with vitamin D, but it is often not enough to meet your daily requirement. Other fortified foods such as orange juice, soy milk, and cereal can provide vitamin D. It is unlikely that you will meet your daily requirement of vitamin D from dietary intake alone and a supplement is recommended. You might find it beneficial to take a greater dosage of vitamin D in the fall or winter, and then lower your dosage in the spring or summer.

Store up some summer sun

The sun is still needed to convert the vitamin D in your body into a usable form. Your body can store some vitamin D in fat cells for the winter. One study links summer sun exposure with vitamin D levels in the winter. How much sun exposure is necessary depends on how dark your skin tone is. According to the Vitamin D Council, the general rule of thumb for adequate sun exposure is "half of the time it takes to turn your skin pink." This might be less than 10 minutes in Miami or one hour in Boston during the summer.

While you might be able to store some of the useable Vitamin D you manufactured during the summer for use during later months, after several weeks with no sun exposure vitamin D levels might be depleted. While sitting in front of a nice bright sunny window will help improve your mood, it is important to note that most glass windows screen out the important ultraviolet B rays your body needs to produce vitamin D.

The latitude where you reside is also an important factor. This poses a problem for those in more northern climates with less sun exposure. In the more northern latitudes, the angle that sun reaches the earth also changes during the winter and unfortunately blocks out most of the necessary ultraviolet B rays. Unfortunately, this means that even if you were streaking naked down a street in Boston during the noon hour in the dead of winter, you would still not get enough sun exposure on your skin to manufacture vitamin D.

Planning a mid-winter vacation to a sunny location will help replenish those reserves. Most light therapy devices do not have ultraviolet B rays, but there are a few lamps designed specifically for vitamin D production, such as the Sperti lamp. Vitamin D is also available as a cream as well.

Vitamin D Deficiency and Other Conditions

Vitamin D, in turn, helps your body absorb calcium. Without enough vitamin D, your body can only absorb 10% to 15% of dietary calcium. Vitamin D is also important in helping to regulate cell growth. Research conducted at Harvard has linked vitamin D deficiency to several types of cancer, including colon, breast, and prostate cancer. Vitamin D deficiency is also linked to osteoporosis, cardiovascular disease, multiple sclerosis, and depression.

Summary on Vitamin D

You need to be taking a vitamin D supplement if you have Seasonal Affective Disorder. Take between 1,000 and 2,000 IUs of vitamin D supplement with your largest meal of the day or with a fatty food to increase absorption. Ideally, take vitamin D with magnesium or also as a combination vitamin. You might find it beneficial to adjust your dosage by talking a larger dosage in the winter and fall months, and decreasing the amount you take in the spring and summer.

Your skin needs some sun exposure to the sun to convert vitamin D into a usable form for your body. Your body can store Vitamin D future use, but your levels do get depleted after several weeks with no sun exposure. Ideally, plan a mid-winter vacation. There are not enough ultraviolet B rays in the northern latitudes during the winter months for your body to manufacture vitamin D, *so even if you streak through Boston during your lunch break*, you will not get enough sun exposure to meet your daily vitamin D requirements.

Vitamin B

There are eight B vitamins referred to as vitamin B complex. They are B1, B2, B3, B5, B6, B7, B9, B12. (Wondering about the missing B vitamins? Apparently B4 is busy playing bingo. B8 and B10 are involved in a round of the board game Battleship, and B11 is playing guitar).

Studies have directly linked B9 and B12 to depression. These B vitamins are also known to be depleted with high alcohol consumption. The results of the study are stated as "On the basis of current data, we suggest that oral doses of both folic acid (800 microg daily) and vitamin B12 (1 mg daily) should be tried to improve treatment outcome in depression."

B9 is also known as folic acid and is found in dark leafy greens, asparagus, beets, beans, and salmon. Folic acid is also commonly found in fortified breads and cereals. It has well known importance in preventing neurological defects during pregnancy. It is needed to synthesize and repair DNA. A deficiency in vitamin B9 has been noted to make prescription antidepressants less effective.

B12 is also known as cobalamin. Vitamin B12 is involved in the metabolism of every cell in the human body. This includes metabolizing fatty acids and amino acids. The study also notes that high levels of B12 are directly associated with better treatment outcomes for those suffering from depression. B12 is found only in animal products, which means many vegetarians are deficient in B12. It is generally found in fish, shellfish, eggs, and pork.

Multivitamin or Vemma

Rather than stressing out about each individual vitamin, it might be more helpful to focus on finding a good overall multivitamin that contains most of your basic daily requirements.

I have found an excellent nutritional drink that I drink every day. It contains high levels of the important vitamins for Seasonal Affective Disorder including vitamins B6, B12, and D. It contains many others important ingredients, too, including vitamins C and E.

I have simplified my life by drinking a Vemma Bode Pro Burn every morning. I buy the cans already made and pop them open like a soda. I have them shipped to my house on auto delivery. For me, they are worth the money. I am not mixing anything or lacking any ingredients to blend. There might be other nutritional drinks out there with similar ingredients, and I have tried many. This one happens to work really well for me, and it contains many of the vitamins that can help with SAD.

It is made with reverse osmosis water, and the protein used is not soy or whey but is made from pea protein. This is important for anyone who has allergies to dairy or soy. It has 20 grams of protein, 7 grams of fiber, and 110 calories. There might be other nutritional protein and vitamin drinks out there, but I have not found one quite as good as Bode Pro Burn from an ingredients and taste perspective. It not only helps with my Seasonal Affective Disorder, but also my weight management issues.

I know I am getting the key nutrients my body needs while saving money on individual supplements. Unfortunately, these are not sold in stores and you must order them from a website. Visit

98

SEASONAL AFFECTIVE DISORDER TREATMENT

http://TheHappySun.com/Vemma for more information on where to purchase.

The Miracle of 5-HTP

The Steps Your Body Takes to Make Serotonin

Brain chemicals, such as serotonin, are made from the amino acids found in food with protein. The amino acid tryptophan is found in food such as turkey, chicken, and eggs. After the food is digested, the body converts the amino acid tryptophan into 5-hydroxytryptophan (5-HTP) or kynurenine. 5-HTP is the building block that the body uses to manufacture serotonin and, in turn, melatonin.

Transforming food into the important brain chemical serotonin is a multi-step process. The first step involves eating enough protein-rich foods that contain the amino acid tryptophan. However, there are a few challenges for the human body to create enough serotonin. Digestion issues, such as poor absorption or low enzyme levels, can hinder the process of providing enough of the essential amino acids needed. After digestion, tryptophan enters the bloodstream, where it is carried to the liver or brain for further processing.

In the liver, enzymes are used to convert tryptophan into 5-hydroxytryptophan (5-HTP) or kynurenine. Stress can actually cause the body to release cortisol, which, in turn, creates more of the liver enzyme that makes kynurenine instead of 5-HTP. Insufficient levels of vitamin B6 and magnesium can inhibit the conversion of tryptophan to 5-HTP. Aspartame or NutraSweet are also known neurotoxins that inhibit serotonin production. Tryptophan can also exit the liver without being converted. Whether tryptophan leaves the liver as 5-HTP, kynurenine, or tryptophan, it enters the bloodstream again and is eventually carried to other parts of the body including the brain.

To enter the brain for further conversion, all amino acids must pass through the blood-brain barrier. The blood-brain barrier prevents harmful chemicals from entering the brain and is thus very selective about which chemicals enter. When tryptophan arrives at the blood-brain barrier, it requires a transport molecule to enter the brain. Tryptophan is then also competing with several other amino acids for a transport molecule. Since tryptophan is one of the smaller amino acids, it is often at the end of the line and does not make it into the brain for processing. Even if you eat a high-protein meal and ingest tryptophan, tryptophan is often beaten out by other amino acids and not able to enter the brain.

If tryptophan is converted into 5-HTP in the liver, it can then more easily pass the blood-brain barrier, where it is then finally converted into serotonin. 5-HTP does not need to wait for a transport molecule because it is more fat-soluble and can easily pass through the blood-brain barrier without a transport molecule.

It seems ironic, then, that low serotonin levels increase cravings for sweet foods and carbohydrates, which generally do not contain the tryptophan. However, this is a way that the body is trying to self-medicate. One reason for this is that if you eat a high-carbohydrate meal, there are less amino acids from protein floating around in the bloodstream waiting for a transport molecule. It allows for more tryptophan to enter the brain to be converted into serotonin.

The high-carbohydrate foods release a quick burst of energy followed by a crash. It sets up a roller coaster ride resulting in further cravings, which can easily lead to weight gain. When your serotonin levels are in balance, cravings are easier to control and you are able to make healthier choices.

5- HTP is Ready-to-Use to Make Serotonin

The most ideal solution to this problem is to take a 5-HTP supplement. When taking 5-HTP as a supplement you are, in fact, skipping several steps in the conversion process of tryptophan. Many people have digestion issues, stress, and vitamin deficiencies that affect the digestion and conversion process of tryptophan, which ultimately results in low serotonin levels. A 5-HTP supplement essentially eliminates these challenges and immediately provides your brain with the building blocks it needs to make more serotonin naturally. Because 5-HTP is a naturally occurring amino acid, it is essentially like eating pre-digested turkey.

Low serotonin is a direct cause of depression, and, specifically, Seasonal Affective Disorder. Having low serotonin levels is also linked to other problems such as alcoholism, ADHD, insomnia, weight issues, PMS, fibromyalgia, chronic fatigue syndrome, and anxiety. 5-HTP is known to help with many issues that low serotonin levels cause, including depression and SAD.

5-HTP has also been known to help curb appetite and help with cravings as part of SAD treatments!

By taking 5-HTP as part of your SAD treatments, you are providing the raw material or building blocks for your body to create its own serotonin naturally. 5-HTP can tried in lieu of an antidepressant to boost mood naturally as part of SAD treatments or treatment for Seasonal Affective Disorder.

5-HTP is Your Personal Helicopter

Just to compare how much more efficient a 5-HTP supplement is in creating serotonin, we can use the analogy of taking a vacation. Think of eating foods with tryptophan as your traditional means of travel, and think of your desired destination as your brain in order to make serotonin. You call a taxi for a ride to the airport (eating food with protein). If there is not enough gas or oil in the taxi (vitamin B or magnesium), you won't even make it to the airport. You might hit traffic along the way (stress) or perhaps a roadblock (aspartame) and even miss your flight. Once you are at the airport, you need to pass through security (absorption) to catch your first plane.

Your first layover spot (liver) is two hours in the wrong direction from your final destination, but it is the best choice for a connecting flight to your desired vacation location. If you are lucky and all goes smoothly, your second flight lands on time. But you then again need a taxi (transport molecule) to get to the final destination. There is a shortage of taxis, as the plane has just landed and lots of other people (amino acids) also need a taxi, and your bags arrived last. A snowstorm in another part of the country could completely delay all of your plans, and you might never even make it. Taking a 5-HTP supplement is the equivalent of having a personal helicopter pick you up at home and fly you directly to your hotel.

5-HTP as a Supplement

To treat Seasonal Affective Disorder, it is recommend that you take 5-HTP up to three times per day for a total of 200 mg to 300 mg. This dosage is if you are not actively taking an antidepressant. It might help appetite cravings if taken 20 minutes before breakfast, lunch, or dinner on an empty stomach, but you can take it with food.

When treating Seasonal Affective Disorder with either 5-HTP or a prescription antidepressant you most likely will need to adjust your dosage by the season. Many SAD patients can even slowly wean off their antidepressants or 5-HTP completely in the spring and summer months. Keep in mind that it does take several weeks for a prescription antidepressant to become effective, so plan ahead for a fall physician's appointment.

If you are taking a prescribed antidepressant, the general advice is to avoid taking 5-HTP, Saint John's Wort, or SAM-e. Combined, they can create the opposite effect of too much serotonin—also known as serotonin syndrome. Symptoms of serotonin syndrome can be mild such as diarrhea, nausea, vomiting, headache, and shivering. Too much serotonin might create anxiety or agitation, or it could cause a person to develop goose bumps or a rapid heart rate. Symptoms can sometimes become severe and cause a high fever, irregular heartbeat, or even seizure. 5-HTP can be used in combination with selective serotonin reuptake inhibitors (SSRIs) when they become ineffective or when a person is weaning off of them. Due to concerns of too much serotonin, it is essential to do so under a physician's supervision.

L-Tyrosine, Gaba, & Other Amino Acids

L-Tyrosine or Dopa Mucuna

Serotonin is only one of many important neurotransmitters in the brain. Dopamine and norepinephrine are other neurotransmitters that can have a strong impact on mood and health. Norepinephrine is manufactured from dopamine. The raw building block to create both dopamine and norepinephrine is an amino acid called L-Tyrosine. Mucuna pruriens is a bean that grows in the tropics. It is very rich in natural L-Dopa. Either L Tyrosine or Dopa Mucuna is available as a supplement.

If 5-HTP alone is not effective in treating Seasonal Affective Disorder, try adding the natural amino acid L- Tyrosine as a supplement as well. Tyrosine is also found in high-protein foods such as beef, fish, and eggs. Low levels of dopamine and, in turn, norepinephrine have been also been noted to be found in those with both Seasonal Affective Disorder and ADHD. L-Tyrosine is also known to help people with thyroid issues. A sluggish thyroid can decrease the effectiveness of 5-HTP or other medications.

If your mood is okay but your energy is severely lacking, you really might benefit from L-tyrosine. This little supplement might just help you get your butt off the couch and get something done. L-tyrosine raises your catecholamines—dopamine, norepinepherine, and adrenaline. These are the sources of your energy, motivation, and focus. L-Tyrosine, which is a naturally occurring amino acid, is also a great supplement to treat ADHD. Generally speaking, it is okay to take 5-HTP and L-Tyrosine (or Dopa Mucuna) together as both are simply amino acids. For safety, however, you might want to consult your physician or pharmacist.

GABA

Gamma-aminobutyric, or more commonly Gaba, is another amino acid supplement worth mentioning because it can be very helpful for those with anxiety issues. It is acts by regulating the firing of neurons and balancing brain chemistry. It inhibits racing thoughts and can be a calming supplement.

Complete Amino Acid Formula

There are 10 essential amino acids and 12 nonessential amino acids. You can go a little crazy trying to figure out which ones to take for what ailment. Poor food quality, digestion and absorption issues, and other factors can lead to a deficiency. Every bone, muscle, and organ is made from a combination of amino acids. They build the neurotransmitters in our brain and play a role in our metabolism and immune system.

For optimal health, it is recommended to take a complete amino acid supplement. A complete amino acid supplement would include L-Tyrosine and Gaba. For the amino acids to be used properly, they generally need the cofactors of vitamin B, calcium, and magnesium as well.

Essential Fatty Acids

Essential fatty acids are an important part of any healthy diet. These healthy fats are called polyunsaturated fats, and they include Omega 3 and Omega 6. Omega 3 fatty acids are found in fish. Omega 6 fatty acids are found in vegetable oils, nuts, and seeds. Unhealthy fats are called saturated fats and are often derived from animals.

Polyunsaturated fats can help reduce bad cholesterol and prevent disease and stroke. These fats are needed to support good brain chemical balance. Our bodies cannot manufacture polyunsaturated fats, so we must obtain them in food.

Technically, Omega 3 can be further categorized into alpha-linolenic acid (ALA), eicosapentaenoic acid (EPA), and docosahexaenoic acid (DHA). Omega 6 can also be further categorized into linoleic acid (LA) and arachidonic acid (AA). There are some detailed discussions that you can find on the Internet debating the ideal ratios of each of these essential fatty acids. Since depression can make you very tired and I don't want you to fall asleep while reading, I will spare you the details concerning that scientific discussion.

The typical American diet is abundant in Omega 6 fatty acids from corn and canola oils. However, such diets often lack in important Omega 3 polyunsaturated fat, which often comes from fish. Certain types of fish have been known to have levels of mercury in them, and mercury is extremely harmful. For this reason, it is important to obtain a quality Omega 3 supplement. The American Heart Association advocates supplementing your diet with Omega 3 fatty acids because of their importance.

Essential fatty acids are important to all humans' health. More interestingly, several studies have shown improvement in depressed patients simply by supplementing their diets with Omega 3 fatty acids.

My guess for us SAD suffers is that we are too busy carb-loading for hibernation and lacking in the healthy fish eating area. If they could make salmon-flavored potato chips that are as delicious as my favorite sour cream and onion potato chips, then I might not need to take fish oil/omega 3 supplements. Since that is not the case, I am telling you that Omega 3 or fish oil is a must-have supplement for Seasonal Affective Disorder.

There is some debate about how much Omega 3 to take, but, on average, it is suggested that you take 1 to 2 grams per day. Your vitamin D is absorbed better when it is taken with a fat, so it is suggested you take both at the same time.

Probiotics

New studies are indicating that probiotics might be helpful for those with depression and anxiety. Probiotics are live bacteria and yeast that found in your body. Having optimal levels of this good bacteria help maintain healthy levels of gut flora, an important factor affecting a person's digestion, immune system, overall health, and mood.

Probiotics help improve digestion and lead to better absorption of important vitamins and minerals. They essentially crowd out more toxic bacteria and even have been thought to aid in helping more tryptophan reach the brain. Tryptophan is the necessary amino acid required to make serotonin. Use of antibiotics can create an imbalance of gut flora. Probiotics are being actively studied as an important supplement, whether you are depressed or not. If you have Seasonal Affective Disorder, you should take a daily probiotic supplement.

Epsom Salt Baths

Epsom salt is magnesium sulfate. It is very inexpensive and can be purchased in the first-aid aisle at most pharmacies. Magnesium is a mineral (not an amino acid) that many people are deficient in. Magnesium and sulfate play an important role in many bodily functions.

An Epsom salt bath is more than just relaxing. It is an effective way for the body to absorb both the magnesium and sulfate it needs through the skin. Epsom salt baths are also thought to be detoxifying and have other health benefits, including aiding sore muscles. Add 2 cups of Epsom salt to a warm bath. If you don't have a bathtub, you might also benefit from a foot bath with Epsom salt.

Melatonin

Melatonin is known as the "sleep hormone." It helps regulate your circadian rhythms, especially when taken at the same time each day. It is beneficial for treating insomnia and other sleep difficulties. Some people with SAD can take melatonin only in the summer months to relax and fall asleep. Some people with Seasonal Affective Disorder can take melatonin all year long, at the same time each night, to help keep their sleep-wake cycle in balance. Melatonin has also been shown to help who suffer from Reverse Seasonal Affective Disorder, or "summer depression." It is available in a liquid form and can be effective for children with sleep issues.

Other natural alternatives:

St. John's Wort or SAM-e

The first suggested treatment for SAD would be the 5-HTP with B vitamins and Omega 3s. If this still is not enough help, the second suggestion would to be to try adding L –Tyrosine. There are two other natural alternatives that you can try: Saint John's Wort or

SAM-e. They are not known to be as effective as 5-HTP but have helped some people with depression or SAD. Please note that you should not be taking 5-HTP, Saint John's Wort, and SAM-e at the same time. It is advisable to consult your doctor regarding any of these alternatives if you are taking prescription antidepressants, because they might raise your levels too high and cause severe adverse reactions with your prescription medication.

Saint John's Wort

Saint John's Wort is a plant that has clusters of yellow flowers. It is considered an herbal remedy. It has been studied and is known to help alleviate mild depression symptoms. It is noted to have antibacterial and antiviral properties. In addition, St. John's Wort has been found to have anti-inflammatory properties.

It can be found in a capsule or extract and is often sold as a tea. For mild depression, dosage is typically suggested to be about 300 mg total per day. It is generally taken three times per day with meals. Caution is advised against using the herb if you are taking prescription antidepressants or are pregnant. It might make ADHD symptoms worse and should not be used with certain medications.

SAM-e

S-Adenosylmethionine (SAM-e) is a naturally occurring molecule found in almost all tissue and fluid in the body. It helps produce and break down brain chemicals, such as serotonin, melatonin, and dopamine. SAM-e works with vitamin B12 and folate (B9). Being deficient in vitamin B12 or folate might reduce levels of SAM-e in your body. SAM-e is also involved in the immune system, and it helps maintain cell membranes and is involved in the process of methylation.

SAM-e has been widely studied for treating osteoarthritis and depression. It has also been used for liver problems and premenstrual and fertility issues.

The recommend dosage of SAM-e is 800–1,600 mg per day orally.

Prescription Antidepressants SSRIs

Popular prescription antidepressant medications are known as SSRIs, which stands for selective serotonin reuptake Inhibitors. Prozac, Zoloft, and Paxil are among commonly prescribed SSRIs. They work much differently than the natural amino acid 5-HTP, which provides the raw material for your brain to create more serotonin. **SSRIs don't create more serotonin. They work by blocking serotonin.**

In your brain, serotonin travels across special nerve cells called neurons. The neurons do not directly touch each other. There is a space between each neuron called a synapse. One neuron has the serotonin and releases it into the synapse to be received by the other neuron. The serotonin binds with the proteins on the receiving cells called receptors. Any serotonin that is left in the synapse during this process is destroyed by enzymes or reabsorbed back into the original neuron to be recycled.

SSRIs work by blocking this recycling process. These drugs prevent the excess serotonin from being reabsorbed back into the original neuron in hopes that more of it will forced to the receiving cell. This increases the amount of serotonin available to receiving neuron, but it decreases the amount of available serotonin from the sending neuron.

When neurons are bombarded with too much serotonin, they eventually change to accommodate this overload. The neurons adapt to the influx by decreasing the number of receptors available to receive serotonin. This process is called downregulation. It also essentially defines how tolerance levels to a drug are built up, and in turn make the drug become ineffective.

The decrease in receptors at the cellular level takes several weeks, which is one reason it takes weeks for an antidepressant to become effective. When your cells change, and your receptors decrease, you are essentially becoming chemically dependent on the drug.

This is another reason why it is critical to slowly wean off SSRIs. The decrease in dosage will give your receptors a chance to slowly rebuild over weeks as you are essentially withdrawing from them. When SSRIs are stopped suddenly, in addition to uncomfortable withdrawal symptoms, it greatly increases a person's suicidal tendencies. Changing medications should be closely monitored by your physician.

Prescription Medications for Seasonal Affective Disorder

Buprorion, commonly sold as Wellbutrin or Zyban, is often prescribed for Seasonal Affective Disorder. Bupropion is a norepinephrine dopamine reuptake inhibitor, or NDRI. This means that Buproprion affects different neurotransmitters than prescription antidepressants that are SSRIs, such as Prozac, Paxil and Zoloft, which primarily impact serotonin only. Buproprion affects the receptors for norepinephrine and dopamine. It is also thought to help with ADHD and have fewer sexual side effects than other antidepressant medications.

- Selective Serotonin Reuptake Inhibitors (SSRIs): Citalopram (Celexa, Cipramil), Dapoxetine Priligy, Escitalopram Lexapro and Cipralex, Fluoxetine Prozac, Fluvoxamine Faverin, Fevarin, Floxyfral, and Luvox), Paroxetine Paxil, Sertraline Zoloft, Lustral.
- Serotonin-Norepinephrine Reuptake Inhibitors (SNRIs): Desvenlafaxine Pristiq, Duloxetine Cymbalta, Milnacipran Savella, Dalcipran, Toledomin, Venlafaxine Effexor, Effexor XR, and Trevilor.
- Norepinephrine-Dopamine Reuptake Inhibitors (NDRIs): Amineptine Survector, Maneon, Directim, Neolior, Provector, Viaspera, Bupropion Wellbutrin and Zyban, Methylphenidate Concerta, Methylin, Medikinet, Ritalin, Equasym XL, Quillivant XR, Nomifensine (Merital, Alival).
- Norepinephrine Reuptake Inhibitors (NRIs): Atomoxetine Strattera, Mazindol Mazanor, Sanorex, Reboxetine (not in USA Prolift or Edronax).

Important: If you currently take prescription antidepressants, do not abruptly stop them. Consult your physician and come up with a plan to gradually lower your dosage and wean off them. Your body can react poorly when you stop taking them quickly, which could worsen your depression or even lead to suicidal feelings.

The difference between 5-HTP & SSRIs

5-HTP is essentially creating more serotonin. It does not interfere with the natural process of reuptaking the excess serotonin back into the original neuron as an SSRI does.

Prescription SSRIs often cause very unpleasant side effects ranging from nausea, dizziness, weight gain, headache, and decreased sexual desire. They can take several weeks to become effective as well. Results from 5-HTP are often seen within a one-week period, and 5-HTP has minimal known side effects.

In one study, 5-HTP raised levels of serotonin by 540%, whereas Paxil, Prozac, and the SSRI raised levels by only 450%, 250%, respectively. Antidepressants, too, can take weeks to become effective.

Consult your physician regarding the appropriate treatment plan for your Seasonal Affective Disorder, as there are times when prescription medications are the most effective way to handle this type of depression—especially if it the patient is unlikely to follow the other treatment suggestions such as light therapy, supplements, and exercise.

Supplement Summary

Supplements can seem overwhelming. It seems like there is a supplement promoted to cure almost every aliment. Some of these are good for overall health, and some of these can make a huge difference in helping to treat the symptoms of Seasonal Affective Disorder. The key is figuring out which ones are effective for you and to take them consistently.

Often, when we start feeling a little less SAD, we start forgetting to take our supplements and inadvertently end up feeling SAD again ... and blaming the supplements for not working. For the speed readers and skimmers, I will try to summarize and categorize the supplements for those with SAD.

Best Bang for Your Buck

5-HTP

5-HTP is a naturally occurring amino acid that your body needs to make serotonin. Serotonin is the neurotransmitter in your brain that balances your moods, and low levels of it lead to depression. For treatment of Seasonal Affective Disorder, it is recommend that you take 5-HTP up to three times per day for a total of 200 to 300 mg.

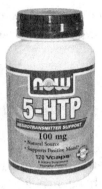

If you are only willing to try one supplement to treat Seasonal Affective Disorder it should be 5-HTP.

Money Very Well Spent

Vitamin B Complex

There is a direct link between depression and low levels of B vitamins in the body. Vitamin B Complex is sold in various forms, both as traditional tablet or capsule supplement and even as a liquid.

Vitamin D

Vitamin D is the "Sunshine Vitamin." If you have Seasonal Affective Disorder, you almost certainly have insufficient levels of this important vitamin. Ideally, take vitamin D with magnesium as vitamin D is often sold as a combination vitamin with the magnesium included.

Read the label of the brand you purchase for suggested dosage, but generally take between 1,000 and 2,000 IUs with your largest meal of the day or with a fatty food to increase absorption.

Pretty Much Everyone Needs These Anyway

Multivitamin or Vemma

Rather than stressing about each individual vitamin, it might be more helpful to focus on finding a good overall multivitamin that contains most of your basic daily requirements.

I have found an excellent nutritional drink that I drink every day. It contains high levels of the important vitamins to treat Seasonal Affective Disorder, including vitamins B6, B12, and D. It also contains many other important ingredients, including vitamins C and E. It has 20 grams of protein, 7 grams of fiber, and 110 calories.

I have simplified my life by drinking a Vemma Bode every morning. I buy the cans and pop them open like a soda in the morning. I have them shipped to my house on auto delivery. For me, they are worth their money. I am not mixing anything or lacking any ingredients to blend. I know I am getting the key nutrients my body needs, while saving money on individual supplements.

Unfortunately, these drinks cannot be found in stores and you must order them from a website. Visit **http://TheHappySun.com/Vemma** for more information on where to buy. I have been reading about vitamins and health for years, and this is one of the best products I have found.

Essential Fatty Acids

Essential fatty acids are an important part of any healthy diet. This healthy fat is also known as Omega 3 and Omega 6. Our diets often have sufficient Omega 6, but tend to lack in Omega 3 which is found in fish oil. A fish oil supplement is suggested for those with SAD, and such a supplement will help vitamin D to be absorbed more easily if you take both together.

Probiotics

These good gut bacteria have an excellent publicist and are commonly being promoted now. Supplementing with probiotics will help crowd out the more toxic bacteria in the gut. New research links probiotics to aiding in the relief of depression and anxiety.

Other Supplements to Help Combat SAD

L-Tyrosine, GABA, or Complete Amino Acid

L -Tyrosine is an amino acid that helps raise dopamine levels and might help with thyroid or ADHD issues. Gaba is a calming amino acid that can help anxiety. Rather than trying to figure out which of the other 20 amino acids you might be lacking, consider taking a complete amino acid blend supplement that contains L-Tyrosine, Gaba, and more.

Melatonin

Melatonin helps regulate your sleep-wake cycle. It can be used to help with sleep difficulties and to reset your internal body clock.

Saint John's Wort or SAM-e

Saint John's Wort or SAM-e might also be helpful in the treatment of Seasonal Affective Disorder. It is this author's opinion that 5-HTP is the more effective treatment, and I would consider one of these other two supplements as alternatives.

Epsom Salt Bath

Epsom salt baths are relaxing and good for your skin. Epsom salt is magnesium sulfate, which can be absorbed through your skin and is important for many bodily functions. Known to help in detoxifying your body, Epsom salts are very inexpensive and can be found at most pharmacies. A warm soothing bath certainly can't hurt with winter depression.

Seek Professional Medical Advice

Supplements can be effective in treating your Seasonal Affective Disorder symptoms. Please read the labels on any supplements you purchase, and follow the manufacturers' guidelines. However, this information I am providing you with here is not intended to be medical advice. This information is intended to be a guide for discussion with your medical professional.

SAD Strategies for

Weight Management

Don't Start on New Year's Day

New Year's Day is *not* the day to start a diet if you have SAD. Let's be honest, it is literally the peak of your funk. You have been completely deprived of that glorious warm natural sunlight for months and have depleted your vitamin D levels down to those of a vampire with osteoporosis. You have the energy of a sloth, and vegetables honestly taste like there are filled with poison in the dead of the winter.

Please note that this is not an all-out excuse to binge eat yourself out of every pair of non-elastic waistband pants you own. I am simply suggesting that you don't set yourself up for failure with the unrealistic expectations of following the latest high-protein or raw food diet to perfection simply because you bought a new calendar. Carbohydrate cravings are a strong and powerful reality for people with Seasonal Affective Disorder.

Progress, not Perfection

Many of us have an "all or nothing" attitude, which can hurt our chances of success with any of our goals. For example, let's say that on day three of your new clean diet you accidentally discover a hidden box of cookies while cleaning out your closet. Before you even have a chance to think about it, you have accidentally inhaled a few cookies while in an almost-possessed trance. At this point, most of us consider the diet over and rather than recovering from the momentary lapse, we forge forward with our new found freedom to eat, and are now shoveling more delicious junk food down our throat, while simultaneously changing into yoga pants.

If you have Seasonal Affective Disorder, let me make the suggestion of using March 1st, or the first day of spring, to start a new diet not January 1st. You will have a little more biological control over your cravings and increase your chances of success.

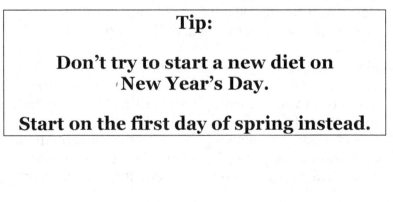

Tip:

Don't try to start a new diet on New Year's Day.

Start on the first day of spring instead.

Why do I crave carbs in the winter?

Chances are that if you have Seasonal Affective Disorder, then the popular "no carb" diets have proved to be absolute torture for you. While you might have some success on these diets in the spring or summer, our bodies physically crave these comforting carbs especially in the winter. This is because these foods have a medicinal effect on us in that they are attempting to raise our serotonin levels.

The problem lies in the fact that those of us with SAD tend to grab the wrong types of food, especially in the late afternoon as the sun begins to set. Candy, pasta, and white bread provide a quick fix by instantly releasing sugar. These types of carbs then have a rebound effect due the drastic spike in our blood sugar and insulin after eating them, which is quickly following by a step drop and further cravings.

You are probably already aware of that fact and **want** to make healthier choices, but insufficient serotonin levels can limit your impulse control. Generally, there is a short time between the urge and your reaction. With low serotonin levels, it is almost biologically impossible to say no. Serotonin controls both mood and appetite. If your serotonin levels are low, your body tries to signal you in the form of cravings to provide what it needs. In essence, your body is trying to self-medicate with food to get more tryptophan. It then uses the tryptophan to make 5-HTP, which is then used to make serotonin. Tryptophan in an amino acid found in high-protein foods such as turkey and fish.

Amino Acid Tryptophan Creates Serotonin

The amino acid tryptophan is needed to manufacture serotonin. Tryptophan is actually found in protein. *So why do we crave carbs and not protein?* This one is a little tricky to answer, but I am glad you asked!

It seems ironic that low serotonin levels increase cravings for sweets foods and carbohydrates, which generally do not even contain tryptophan. The answer lies in how the body processes amino acids. Amino acids need a transport molecule to cross the blood brain barrier. *Unlike our parents who love us all equally, transport molecules actually have "favorite" amino acids, and unfortunately tryptophan is not one of them.*

In Hollywood terms, consider tryptophan as B-List actor (or amino acid) compared with the other more famous and important actors (or amino acids). All of these actors need an escort (transport molecule) down the red carpet into the Oscars (your brain). The other more famous actors (amino acids) keep getting escorted in first, and tryptophan is still stuck outside waiting to get in after the show has started.

Tryptophan is there because you have eaten some protein earlier, but it can't get into the big event (your brain) because all the escorts are busy. Carbohydrates and sugar release insulin. Insulin's job is to remove sugar from the blood and escort it into cells to be used as energy. Insulin also transports amino acids into muscle cells, where the amino acids are then used for protein synthesis to build muscle. This quick spike in blood sugar, acts as a distraction to some degree, sending the other amino acids off to the muscles, making it easier for tryptophan to hitch a ride into our brains.

Back to our Hollywood analogy, a Hollywood bodyguard is a transport molecule. It escorts all the Hollywood elite amino acids over to specific areas of the red carpet for photographs and interviews with the paparazzi (muscles). While the elite Hollywood amino acids are busy posing with the distraction of the paparazzi, insulin is now available to escort tryptophan quickly and easily into the big event (brain) since the paparazzi is not interested in little old tryptophan. In addition if a high-carbohydrate meal is eaten, then there are less amino acids from protein floating around in the bloodstream waiting for a transport molecule. A higher-carbohydrate meal allows for more tryptophan to enter the brain and, in turn, be converted into serotonin.

Now if the carbohydrates consumed are mostly simple sugars, these carbohydrates break down fast and cause a huge spike and start a roller coaster effect. These simple sugars release a quick burst of energy, which is followed by a crash. It sets up a roller coaster ride, resulting in further cravings as your body tries to stabilize. Clearly this pattern can easily lead to weight gain. Complex carbohydrates and fiber help stabilize this pattern because they break down more slowly.

Poor diets that are low in protein do not provide the body with enough tryptophan. High-protein diets limit the body's ability to convert tryptophan into 5-HTP. Restrictive dieting often causes concentrations of tryptophan in the bloodstream to plummet and also increases the intensity of your cravings. Many people also lack the proper enzymes to convert tryptophan into 5-HTP once it reaches the brain even if they are eating a balanced diet. The lack of serotonin results in strong carbohydrate cravings is also part of the root cause of both obesity and bulimia.

Bottom line is your body *needs* serotonin. It *craves* serotonin. It will create unhealthy cravings for sugar to just to get a quick fix of serotonin. Why not make it easy, and give your body what it wants? 5-HTP is really just like eating turkey that has already been converted from tryptophan to the building block for serotonin. Taking 5-HTP supplements will help you gain the control to make healthier eating choices and limiting carb cravings because your body has what it wants.

One final thought here in Hollywood: What happens when that B-list actor finally lands his award-winning role? In essence, this is what happens when tryptophan is converted into 5-HTP. 5-HTP is the equivalent of Hollywood royalty and does not require an escort into the Oscars or your brain. In fact, taking a 5-HTP supplement is equivalent to having a personal helicopter fly the celebrity directly to the event. They waltz right in for their role in the show.

Please tell me that this Hollywood analogy helped you understand your brain chemicals, and carb cravings a little better? If so, thank the academy by leaving a 5-star review of this book.

You Need a Summer Diet and a Winter Diet

Because of the biological changes that happen to those of us with Seasonal Affective Disorder, it makes sense that we need to adapt with the seasons. People with SAD tend to crave more carbohydrates and sweets during the winter. You will have better success losing weight during the other seasons.

Freeze Ahead Meals

During the winter, focus on trying to prepare some freeze-ahead meals. The concept behind freeze-ahead meals is to prepare several meals in bulk on one day to save time, money and energy cooking later. Many of them can go right from your freezer in the morning to a crockpot so dinner will be ready and waiting for you after work. Find a few good recipes and then make a grocery list on a blah wintery day. Then when the sun comes out (or after light therapy) when you are in a better mood, run to the store and immediately spend a little time prepare several meals you can freeze and eat later.

I had stumbled across this concept a while back with an article that promised I would not need to cook for a month. While I am not that efficient enough to have a 30 day supply of meals on hand, I have found spending a little time preparing on a good day makes my life much easier on my off days.

Freeze-ahead meals are much better strategy than my previous game plan in which I would open the freezer door after I am already starving, blankly stare at the frozen meat like it is a UFO (unidentified frozen object), sit down only to repeat this door opening and staring process several more times, and eventually order a pizza after devouring a half a bag of chips trying to make a decision.

Random Author's Comment:

If you are making freeze ahead crockpot meals and are storing them in a Ziplock bag, I have a tip for you. Try to fold the Ziplock bag in such a manner that your meal freezes to a size that will fit in your crockpot. I *may* have learned this lesson the hard way when I was rushing out the door one morning and *attempting to microwave defrost a very large frozen rectangle of beef tips and gravy that clearly did not fit in my crockpot.*

My best advice is to not attempt to undertake a low-carb or no-carb diet during the winter. In my opinion, you are setting yourself up for unrealistic expectations due to the strong carb cravings. Allow yourself some comfort foods, but try to focus more on reasonable portion control during the winter. Winter is the season for pot roast in the crockpot. Visit TheHappySun.com/Store for a list of some great freeze ahead cookbooks or find them directly on Amazon.com.

During the spring and summer, cut back on the starchy carbs. Focus on eating more fresh fruits and vegetables and protein. Think summer salads and shrimp or steak on the grill.

Stop Focusing on Strict Diet Rules

I have spent way too much time attempting to follow dietary rules instead of listening to what my body needs. It was a major breakthrough for me when I finally realized that my body's dietary needs change with the seasons. Understanding this is important to your success. You might find it helpful to break up your diet and exercise plans into four three-month cycles and adapt them to the seasons.

There are a million different diets with all types of rules. I really hate when I attempt to follow one of these plans and have *never even heard of half of the ingredients.* If I have to google the ingredients and conduct a scavenger hunt through my local grocery then chances are that I will not be following that plan long term. *I may or may not be a "drop-out" of many different diet plans.*

Obviously the cleaner you eat, the better. Your body needs protein, carbohydrates, and fats to survive. What ratio, diet, or rules you want to follow to achieve that goal it entirely up to you. I hope to offer you some general dietary guidelines to help with your struggle against Seasonal Affective Disorder. Your specific food choices are entirely up to you.

Fill up on Fiber and The Elephant Yam

Fiber

Fiber comes from fruits and vegetables. It is an indigestible part of the plant, and it passes through our systems as bulk material or roughage. It has important health benefits, including weight loss. Fiber keeps your bowel movements regular and helps maintain healthy cholesterol. It also has a key role in preventing a number of major illnesses, including diabetes, heart disease, stroke, cancer, and obesity.

Fiber helps stabilize your blood sugar and insulin levels. It basically slows the rate at which food enters your bloodstream. This helps create balance and control cravings. Fiber evens out the drastic roller coaster ride created by sugar and simple carbohydrates. It literally fills you up so you are not constantly feeling hungry. It keeps things moving through your digestive tract and helps eliminate toxins.

There are two types of fiber—soluble and insoluble. Soluble fiber dissolves in water and becomes more of a gelatin. Insoluble fiber does not dissolve in water. Both have benefits, but it is recommended to have more soluble fiber overall.

The recommended daily amount of fiber for women is 25 grams and men its 38 grams, according to the Academy of Nutrition and Dietetics. The typical American diet averages only 10–12 grams of fiber per day, and I'm sure that number is lower in the winter for those with the winter blues.

Food sources of soluble fiber include kidney beans, pinto beans, Brussels sprouts, broccoli, spinach, zucchini, apples, oranges, grapefruit, grapes, prunes, oatmeal, and whole-wheat bread. Food sources of insoluble fiber include vegetables—especially dark leafy greens, root vegetable skins, fruit skins, whole wheat products, wheat bran, corn bran, nuts, and seeds. They also make high-fiber and high-protein shakes.

During a gorgeous spring or summer day, I love putting vegetables on the grill outside or having a great salad for lunch. I am motivated to have healthy snacks.

I'll be honest. Vegetables just don't taste good to me in the winter. They taste sour. Of course, this might be because they are often rotting and buried in the back of the drawer in my fridge. Plus fresh vegetables are at the grocery store, which I am not motivated to visit because it is cold and dark, and I am already home after a long tiresome winter day.

Elephant Yam

Because I do not get enough of my fiber from vegetables in the winter, I have a secret weapon for weight management for those with Seasonal Affective Disorder. It is called Glucomannan. It is fiber extracted from konjac root, also called elephant yam.

Glucomannan is a natural soluble fiber that has been well studied. It is often an ingredient in other health products such as the supplement PGX. PGX also contains xanthan gum and sodium alginate. Sodium alginate is extracted from brown seaweed and used as a thickener in food products such as pudding or jam.

Sold as glucomannan or konjac root, this fiber is relatively inexpensive. Sold as PGX or under other brand names with other ingredients, it can be much more expensive. Glucomannan is generally more well tolerated than other fiber supplements such as psyllium, which can often cause abdominal cramps and gas. Psyllium is also derived from a grain, which can be problematic for some.

You will want to start off slow with any fiber supplement and drink plenty of water. Typically, the brand you buy will offer a suggested number of capsules to take approximately a half hour before each meal. For example the Now Foods brand of Glucomannan suggests taking three capsules of 575 mg (1,725 mg total) with at least 8 oz. of water. During your first week or two, to avoid any gastrointestinal distress, I would suggest taking only half of that amount or less until your body adjusts to the new volume of fiber.

> # Bottom Line:
>
> ## To prevent yourself from becoming an elephant over the winter use glucomannan or elephant yam.

Breakfast with Protein

Within One Hour

If you do not eat within the first hour of waking up, your body assumes that you are going into starvation mode. After all, you haven't eaten for the several hours you were asleep. Your body will then release beta-endorphins, which are natural pain killers, to prevent you from the pain of starvation. You might not realize this, but it feels good to not eat breakfast, at least for a little while. Many people think that they are not hungry and go straight for the caffeine in coffee for an added little burst. Unfortunately, this pattern sets you up for a challenging day biochemically.

You are basically climbing the first big-lift hill of the daily roller coaster by skipping breakfast. If you wait too long, you end up with a strong craving for something with sugar or a simple carbohydrate that can break down quickly in your body. This, in turn, causes your insulin levels to rise very quickly. Your blood sugar comes crashing down shortly afterward, causing a craving to boost it again. This creates a drastic up-and-down pattern for your day that becomes difficult to stabilize when in set motion.

Find a Protein Drink

The goal of eating breakfast with protein within one hour of waking up is to stabilize your blood sugar and brain chemistry for the day, so you have less cravings and more control over what you eat later on. For me, the easiest way I can accomplish this goal is with a protein drink. I am not dragging my butt out of bed each winter morning and cooking eggs every day.

I drink a protein drink that a company called Vemma makes. I drink the Vemma Bode Pro Burn drink in the red can every single morning in spring, summer, fall, and winter. It has 20 grams of protein made from peas and rice protein. It does not contain gluten or soy. It is full of the daily vitamins I need and even made with reverse osmosis water. I order it online and it is shipped to my home automatically every month. I order it already made in the can. There is a less-expensive version of the product where you add your own water. I personally would rather just pop open a can every morning. It works for me.

My best advice for weight management with Seasonal Affective Disorder is for you to find a protein drink you like and drink it daily. If you do this within the first hour of waking up you will start each day off on the right foot from a biochemical perspective. It will give you more control to continue to make healthier choices later in the day and result in less cravings. I am going to add that I am an affiliate of Vemma because I believe in their products. Whether you choose Vemma Bode Burn or another protein drink is entirely up to you. I am simply letting you know what works for me. Either way, **breakfast with protein within one hour of waking is important**.

Unfortunately, these drinks are not found in stores and you must order them from a website. I have been reading about vitamins and health for years, and this is one of the best products I have found.

Visit **http://TheHappySun.com/Vemma**.

Breakfast Carbs in the Winter

After your protein drink, you should still have breakfast of some sort or a mid-morning snack. There is much debate about certain foods being healthy enough. My guess is that if you have SAD, that you are not eating that well during the winter. Cut yourself a little slack from being a perfectionist. Follow stricter diets in the spring and summer.

Allow yourself to have some carbs in the winter. Try to choose high-fiber products, if possible. There are many high-fiber English muffins, granola bars, and oatmeals from which to choose. They figured out a way to sneak fiber into cottage cheese too, which is a good source of protein even by itself. They are some great baking mixes to make high-fiber pancakes and muffins too.

I like Kashi products. They have healthy ingredients. They make some excellent cereals, such as "Go Lean" and "Go Lean Crunch," that have both protein and fiber. They also make frozen waffles and granola bars. For a quick lunch, they make frozen entrees. The Chicken Florentine and Sweet and Sour Chicken are great. I am a fan of their thin crust pizza because a just few minutes in the oven, I am eating guilt free!

The great thing about fiber is that it inherently it fills you up and tends to be lower in calories. It helps stabilize your blood sugar so that you are not quickly crashing and searching for more food, as happens with our highly processed food choices. There are a lot of great options out there now that help fill the need for those cozy winter carbs!

Having some protein at dinner also provides the body with the basic building blocks it needs to make happy brain chemicals at night.

How to Make Healthy Eating Easy

I am going to give a quick shout out to a new online marketplace to order healthy, organic food right to your doorstep. I am advocate of this program because it makes healthy eating easy and affordable. I will disclaim that I am also an affiliate of this program as well and I use it. As they so eloquently describe it:

"Thrive Market is the first socially conscious online marketplace offering the world's best-selling natural and organic products at wholesale prices. Think Costco meets Whole Foods online."

My goal is to provide you with a few key resources for Seasonal Affective Disorder and to help you improve your overall health. I like healthy food that shows up at my doorstep, however I don't want you to feel like you are reading commercials. If you want to learn more about why I advocate for this program, you can read a more detailed description at

http://TheHappySun.com/ThriveMarket.

Summary

To summarize the key points of this chapter, my best advice on managing your weight with Seasonal Affective Disorder includes:

- Don't start a new diet on New Year's Day
- Your body needs carbohydrates
- Have different diet plans for the different seasons
- Prepare for winter with freeze ahead meals
- Eat breakfast with protein within one hour of waking (protein drink)
- Fill up on fiber or supplement with glucomannan
- Stop trying to follow diets with strict crazy rules
- Make eating healthy easy for your lifestyle

That's the *skinny* on this chapter!

Moving Beyond the Light

Light therapy gets all the glory in treating Seasonal Affective Disorder. It is the most popular and widely discussed treatment option. It alone is not a complete and total cure for SAD however. The vitamins and amino acids discussed in the previous chapter will help balance your brain chemicals. There are a few other things that can help ease the discomfort of your winter symptoms as well.

The Magic of Music

Imagine that it is a warm and gorgeous summer day. You are cruising in your car and there is absolutely no traffic. You are just driving around enjoying your freedom and the amazing weather. You feel absolutely wonderful! The radio is cranking out one good song after another!

What songs do you hear on your radio? What songs make you feel alive?

You have my permission now to go to Amazon Digital Music or wherever you buy music and download some of those songs now. I want you to create a little playlist of upbeat music that makes you feel happy and alive. Songs that make you feel like moving, dancing, and singing.

Set yourself up so you can listen to your music easily. This might mean that you invest in a portable music device or figuring out how to use the Amazon Cloud to synch your music across multiple devices. Perhaps you can create a CD to leave in your car for when you are driving to work or you can download the songs to your smart phone. Keep headphones at your desk so you can listen at work. Just set yourself up so you can surround yourself with *your music* quickly and easily.

Music has a powerful affect on us. It alters your brain waves. It moves us physically, mentally, and spiritually. The point is to use music to help you feel better naturally. Music is very personal and different for everyone. Find music that moves you and that makes you feel alive.

Need ideas for your playlist? Think back to your childhood or teenage years. I know there are songs that make you smile. Check out the Best Sellers lists for current hits.

Move Your Body

Now that you have your tunes turned on, let's talk about moving your body ... Stop. I heard you groan.

Winter Exercise Versus Summer Exercise

First, let's be realistic. You have Seasonal Affective Disorder and I understand that you move slower than snail stuck in molasses in January. You physically change with the seasons. Your winter exercise plan should be different than your spring exercise plan. New Year's Day is not the time to start an aggressive exercise routine if you have SAD. You have my permission to delay your New Year's resolutions until March. Hopefully this lightning bolt of an idea makes sense to you and allows you to stop beating yourself up for past resolutions gone awry, but you do need to move your body some during the winter.

Think of it this way: Your favorite sports team has an offensive plan and a defensive plan. Imagine the spring and summer seasons as your offense, where you are taking charge and scoring points in life. This analogy would clearly make winter your defensive season. You need one plan for exercise in the winter and a different and more energetic plan to exercise in the spring and summer months.

Just like in sports, you need to adjust your strategy depending upon which team you are playing against. In the winter you will need to work harder, and follow your treatment plan, and yet you still might not make much progress. Summer is easy and an almost effortless victory for those of us with Seasonal Affective Disorder. Winter is a harder team to beat. You need a different strategic plan for each.

"Exercise! You are saving your endangered endorphins!"

~Jozzie Ray

Exercise has a powerful effect on our body, mind, and mood. Exercise releases endorphins in your brain that make you feel good. These endorphins have been shown to reduce stress and anxiety levels. Endorphins also help alleviate pain and sensitivity. You are more sensitive and your body physically experiences more pain when you don't exercise. Studies have proved that exercise helps alleviate depression. *However, I do understand the complete irony of being too depressed to exercise.*

Walking in a Winter Wonderland

I know. I know. It is hard to exercise when it is cold and dark outside and you have no energy. You are tired. I get it. I am not suggesting starting high-intensity training or a boot camp type routine right now. I am just talking about getting some regular movement going in your life, such as maybe walking a few times per week or a doing a half-hour exercise show on the television and fast forwarding through the commercials. It is important to keep you from crashing and burning even further into depression.

Step 1: USE YOUR MUSIC TO MOTIVATE YOU TO EXERCISE! Get your favorite playlist cranking!

Think small at first. Maybe day one is simply removing the laundry from the treadmill and dusting it off or trying to find your portable music player. Try to envision yourself exercising. What seems fun or at least doable for you? Be realistic. Seasonal Affective Disorder makes you want to stay home and hide under the covers. It might not be a smart idea to join a gym that you are never going to want to drive to during the winter. Perhaps the most realistic option is an exercise DVD that you can do at home or walking on the treadmill while using your light therapy box.

Walking is easy and natural. If you can initially aim for 20 minutes per day three times a week, you will be heading in the right direction. Break it up into two 10- to 15-minute segments per day if you need to. You don't even have to change clothes or worry about when to take your shower if you just simply walk. (I know you are using those as excuses not to exercise... because I do to. Now stop over thinking and get your butt on that treadmill!) Once you get going, you will notice that exercise does boost your mood and energy level.

I do best when I walk two miles a day. On good weather days, my neighbors are used to seeing me walking around the block twice. In the winter, I try to set up my light box in front of the treadmill and grab my music. I promise myself that I will at least do 15 minutes. I usually find that once I get started, I have more energy and can keep going. I can walk any time of day and not worry about sweating, what I am wearing, when I should shower or any other random excuse I can think of.

Don't over think your exercise plan.

Turn on your music.

Then just start moving.

Spring Forward

Spring naturally revitalizes us. We begin coming back to life. We have more bounce in our step. We might even become a little *too hyper* and bounce off the walls. This can be part of having Seasonal Affective Disorder. Try to notice what time of year this happens for you and plan for it. Take advantage of this extra energy and optimize on it.

This is the time to start a more regimented exercise routine. You will have the motivation and discipline to follow through with your plan more easily. You will naturally begin to crave healthier foods, and it should be easier to lose weight. Use this part Seasonal Affective Disorder to your advantage.

Try to fit in some higher intensity interval training a few times per week in the spring. Those short spurts of getting your heart rate up will help you lose weight faster. Now is the time to join the gym or sign up for those boot camp style classes. You will likely appreciate the socialization and the exercise if you do. Consider the spring solstice as your New Year's Eve and time to start your resolutions. It is your good season. Go for it!

Ditch the All-or-Nothing Mindset

I want you to change your mindset. We can tend to be "all or nothing" people. We are either following some strict diet and regimented exercise routine or completely off the bandwagon. *If everyone stayed put on the bandwagon, then they wouldn't need keep inventing "new diets" and exercise programs for people to try.*

I am trying to be realist. We are going to have good days and weeks and bad days and weeks, but we need to keep trying to get in some exercise. If you start off too fast, you might burn out and quickly quit the whole thing. We all have a tendency to be gung-ho in the beginning and quickly fizzle. Consistent exercise is the best way to get those much-needed endorphins on a daily basis.

Exercise needs to become part of your daily routine where you don't feel complete without it. You will have off days and even off weeks, but if you ditch your supplements, stop sitting in front of your light, and stop exercising, well then quite frankly you are going to quickly find yourself back in a major slump. You don't completely give up on brushing your teeth forever just because you forget to do it one morning.

Adjust Your Attitude and Expectations

Part of the problem with Seasonal Affective Disorder is attitude and expectations, of both ours individually and of society's as a whole. There is an expectation that we are supposed to be perfectly in balance at all times, and moving in a forward progression. We neglect the ebb and flow of nature. There are high tides and low tides. Seasons change. Think of all the different types of plants and trees out there and how not all of them can survive in certain zones or conditions. Not everyone understands Seasonal Affective Disorder, but if you have it, it is important that you educate yourself and understand how it affects you personally.

An Analogy For Friends and Family

The Sugar Maple Versus the Pine Tree

Some people are like sugar maple trees and their leaves turn vibrant beautiful colors, but then those beautiful leaves die and fall off during the winter. Sugar maples then regrow their leaves in the spring and they provide shade during the summer.

Other people are like pine trees and are stable and green all year long. Pine trees may not understand why sugar maple trees make such a dramatic fuss and change their leaves all different colors. Pine trees may think sugar maple tree should stay green all year just like they do, but you can't simple talk a tree out of changing the color of its leaves. It is naturally responding to its environment.

Even if you reason with a sugar maple tree and thoroughly explain why it should keep it's leaves green all winter, it will still go through the dramatic process of changing the color of its leaves. The sugar maple tree may hate that it behaves like this and wish it were stable like a pine tree, but it cannot control it's leaves from a biochemical reaction based on the environmental conditions.

You can try to "cure" a sugar maple tree, or "treat" it, by putting it in a greenhouse and giving it lots of warmth and light during the winter. This might keep its leaves green for that winter, but biologically it is still a sugar maple tree.

We focus too much on the leaves dying or not being green all year like a pine tree. We need to focus on the shade sugar maple trees provide and the beautiful artistic colors it can produce. People pay money, and plan vacations just to see the amazing colors these trees produce in the fall.

Sugar maple trees are different. They are special. They create art. Those of us that change so vibrantly with the seasons due to Seasonal Affective Disorder are the sugar maple trees in life. One tree is beautiful, but a forest full of those of us living healthy lives with Seasonal Affective Disorder is spectacular!

Pine trees might never understand sugar maple trees ... but, hey, pine trees are the ones decorated in artificial lights at Christmas!

Maybe ... Just Maybe ...

It is Time to Move:

My Story

Hot apple cider, crisp cool air, and a cozy warm sweater coupled with the distinct rustling sound of a kaleidoscope of leaves shuffling beneath your feet are the images that paint the portrait of an idealistic autumn afternoon in New England. Honestly, I love the fall, but I also know it is the time of year that I begin to slowly start to suffocate.

I was born and raised in a small town in central Massachusetts. It was the type of town where everyone knew everyone else because not only had they lived there their entire lives, but many of their parents and grandparents had also been born and raised there too, including mine. I had some of the same school teachers who taught my parents decades before. I graduated in a class of less than one hundred students, the majority of whom had been my classmates since kindergarten. People just didn't to move much.

I first learned that I had Seasonal Affective Disorder when I was in high school. It was a topic on an Oprah episode. Ironically I was home to see the show because *for some reason* I had quit the basketball team. I knew how I felt in the winter, and I witnessed my mother struggle with depression in the years before anyone knew what Prozac was. I felt some relief to have a name for what I felt. I also wanted to know the "cure" for Seasonal Affective Disorder.

I made serious plans to go to college in North Carolina. I knew I wanted to move somewhere warmer, but I never made it. Instead I met the man who turned out to be my husband, and he lived in a neighboring town in Massachusetts. Ultimately, I chose to stay up north. We eventually bought a house together and had two beautiful babies. Both our families were nearby, which we truly enjoyed.

However year after year, I went through the same cycle with my Seasonal Affective Disorder. The month of September usually brought about a sense of restlessness and irritability. I would usually change something major in my life; often my job. I could feel the weight of my depression start to creep in. I would try with all my life to fight it off, kicking and screaming. Eventually my struggle would fade like a tired toddler at the end of a tantrum and I would simply become a shell of my former self. Chronic exhaustion swept in like a thick fog encompassing my every action making the most mundane tasks felt like insurmountable obstacles. That is the realty of winter depression.

During my worst year with Seasonal Affective Disorder, all I could think about was driving south. It was a deep primal urge to flee or escape in order to survive. It was a thought that next to impossible to ignore. I had two young toddlers at home and was getting very little sleep. I felt like a shell of a human forcibly dragging myself through the bare minimum of motions that I needed to do, and yet somehow failing at even those.

Each morning, when my husband left for work, I remember thinking that if I just got in the car and started driving south that I could be below the Mason-Dixon line with the kids by the time he got home. I didn't have a plan, but I knew that in just eight hours I could be somewhere warmer and brighter. Every cell in my body wanted to migrate south. I didn't want to leave him, my home, or my family, but each day felt like an eternity that winter. I was so uncomfortable in my own skin, and my body ached because it craved to get what it desperately needed—sun.

I did not leave that year, but after much encouragement from friends and family I did finally go see my physician. I remember describing how debilitating Seasonal Affective Disorder had become in my life. We went over prescription medication options and how they would up to take six weeks to work. Unfortunately, I had a very bad reaction to the antidepressant that I was prescribed. It made me extremely hesitant to try another.

I also remember how stunned I was when my physician proposed that maybe I should consider moving south especially since Seasonal Affective Disorder was known to get increasingly worse for women at my age. We had a house, kids, jobs, and family. I just assumed that I had missed my chance in life to move. It seemed ridiculous to move at that point in our lives. Eventually spring came, the snow melted away and so did my depression. I began to feel human again. We stayed in Massachusetts another year.

After that particularly bad winter had finally passed, I found that I was starting to get extremely anxious about the upcoming winters, as early as August. I didn't want to go to that dark place again. I did not want to feel like I was slowly dying. Seasonal Affective Disorder can make you feel like you are being suffocated, with each day giving you a little bit less oxygen. It was an awful sense of anticipation to know the darkness was coming again. My SAD was getting worse each year, and it was a predictable impending doom.

Our lives quickly took an unexpected turn the next summer. The economy started to crash, and it was imminent that my husband was going to be losing his job. He started sending out applications everywhere. I was also working, but my income was not enough to sustain our family. He received a call, an interview, and a job offer in the Virginia Beach area in a matter of one week.

Perhaps if the previous few winters had not have been so bad, we would not have seriously considered that job offer. But they were bad. Worst of all, I knew that my son was also showing signs of suffering from SAD. I would do anything to prevent him or any other human from feeling as bad as I did. Over a whirlwind three-week period, we sold our house, put almost everything we owned in storage, blindsided our families with the news, and left the cold dark winters of Massachusetts behind.

We now live in a military area, and people move in and out all the time. It is a normal part of life. I had been born, raised, had my first apartment, and purchased my first home all within a five-mile radius. I am not cured. I still have my light therapy box and use it late in the winter. However, I no longer need to live by it from October through March like I needed to in Massachusetts.

My family moved south because of Seasonal Affective Disorder. It is better for me here. It is better for my son here too. I believe that moving south saved him from some of the severe struggles I have gone through.

One of the biggest misconceptions is that people think I hate the snow. I actually do love the serenity of watching the snow fall from inside my home. I enjoyed playing in the snow on warmer days. I do hate the biting cold, however. We now live in an area where when we occasionally get snow, and it is funny to me to see the whole city shut down for just an inch of snow.

It has been six years since we moved. I am happier and healthier in the south, though we do miss being around our extended families. I am fortunate because using the techniques I wrote about in this book, my depression has become a fading distant memory. I walk outside the majority of the year. I am grateful to be able to do so. I know walking and exercise is important for my mental health. I take my supplements including 5 HTP, and late in the winter I use my light therapy device.

Friends and family who know my gregarious personality may be surprised to read such dramatic description of depression from a girl they know who loves to make people laugh. I have always been an optimist, and try to focus on the positive in life. The handful of people I let into my life can attest that the descriptions of my depression are sadly accurate, and I thank you personally for being there for me during those difficult times.

To those who haven't experienced the strangling grips of depression, uprooting our lives and moving south might seem extreme. To those who bought this book, maybe this was something you needed to hear as a potential option in your own life.

Ironically, one of the worst thing about moving after all those years is being stuck with a wicked bad Boston accent in the south! No one knows what I'm sayin' down he-ah!

"Some people are like sugar maple trees and their leaves turn vibrant beautiful colors, but then those beautiful leaves die and fall off during the winter.

Other people are like pine trees and are stable and green all year long. Pine trees may never understand why sugar maple trees make such a dramatic fuss... "

~Jozzie Ray

Seasonal Affective Disorder Survival Guide

Real-Life Advice

Chances are you bought this book because you were looking for some answers or solutions for dealing with Seasonal Affective Disorder. I offer you this "cheat sheet" chapter or "SAD Survival Guide." After long winded boring explanations of brain chemicals, I have tried to condense the best of my knowledge in *"living a SAD life"* for you right here.

1. Seasonal Affective Disorder is real.

Your brain chemicals change due to a lack of sunlight. The change in seasons also affects many animals and plants. It is a natural biological reaction. It is the same chemical reaction that causes squirrels to gather nuts, birds to migrate, bears to hibernate. and leaves to change color.

A sugar maple tree has leaves that change from green to yellow to red to brown. The leaves fall off during the winter and regrow again the spring. The lack of sunlight does not affect every plant or animal so drastically, just as Seasonal Affective Disorder does affect every person. Pine trees don't change color in the winter, which is why they make excellent Christmas trees in the winter.

Even if you have the milder version of SAD and just get the "winter blues," it is time that you accept that SAD is part of who you are biologically. It is part of your genetic make-up, and part of who you are naturally. You are not just being a *big baby* about winter. It is literally in your head ... meaning your brain chemicals.

Your family, friends, or co-workers might not fully understand, but it is important that you understand that Seasonal Affective Disorder is *real.*

2. Your symptoms will change with the seasons.

Understand that nature has cycles. There are patterns that escalate and decline in life. Think of the ocean tides rolling in and out or the change of the seasons. We often disappoint ourselves with unrealistic expectations that our lives should be perfectly in balance at all times or consistently progressing forward.

For those of us with Seasonal Affective Disorder, our moods and ability to perform ebb and flow with the change of seasons. We tend to focus solely on the negative feelings of the winter months without realizing the potential benefit that many of us have to be very productive in the spring or summer months. You might need to mentally cut yourself some slack and accept that you tend to be a little less efficient during the winter. Try to limit your obligations during your slow season, if possible, and catch up on things during the spring or summer when you naturally have extra energy.

Setbacks are a natural part of progression. We need to understand that our progress can wax and wane and that if we falter, we simply need to begin to move forward again without jumping off the bandwagon completely. Too often, our society sees things as "all or nothing" without recognizing the true patterns or cycles of life. We might naturally be a little happier if we simply adjust our expectations of ourselves to be more realistic and seasonal.

3. Realize you need at least two game plans.

You physically change because of Seasonal Affective Disorder. Your brain chemistry changes. Your energy levels and mood change with the seasons. You need two playbooks—one for spring and summer and second one for fall and winter. In sports, this is the equivalent to adjusting your strategy depending on whether you are playing offense or defense. Your game plan will be different based upon what type of team you are playing against.

Your life plan should be different in the winter than it is in the summer. You should have different goals for your diet, exercise, and social life during the winter versus the summer. Adjusting your attitude and expectations about your life with Seasonal Affective Disorder is a huge part of this battle. It is not an excuse to do nothing during the winter, but rather a realization that you will need to work harder to follow your treatment plan and still might not make as much progress. Summer is easy and almost effortless. Winter is a harder team to beat. You need a different strategic plan for each.

4. Be proactive.

Seasonal Affective Disorder is pretty predictable. It most likely will be a factor in your life year after year. Some years will be better than others. We spend a lot of time and energy looking for solutions to our problems. Even when we know what will help us, we sometimes neglect to follow the advice or simply wait too long to do so. While our moods and energy might fluctuate naturally, there is no need to completely crash and burn every year.

Schedule a reoccurring annual physician appointment for the mid-fall or for whenever you historically start to feel bad. This way, it will already be on your calendar to discuss your plan of attack for the upcoming winter. You are essentially scheduling time in advance to stop and take care of yourself.

Booking these appointments in advance will also help if you take prescription antidepressants, since they can take several weeks to become fully effective. You might need to take them only during the winter or adjust the dosage seasonally. Stopping your medication suddenly can have a drastic effect and make your depression worse or even lead to suicidal feelings. Follow your physician's advice on dosage and how and when to wean off them.

Address any other co-existing conditions with your physician. Science has proved that people with Seasonal Affective Disorder are also prone to other conditions such as ADHD, bipolar disorder, thyroid issues, weight management issues, or alcohol and drug issues. Discuss treatment for these often related issues during the time with your physician as well.

When we feel good, we are generally not preparing for when we might later feel bad. Since SAD is predictable, we are fortunate to have the opportunity to be proactive. Pick up the phone and make a physician's appointment for this year and next year.

5. Stockpile your nuts for the winter.

Set up your supplements, such as 5-HTP, vitamin D, and melatonin, so that they are automatically delivered to you through a service such as Subscribe and Save from Amazon Prime. Let's face it, automatic delivery is better than driving out to the store in the cold and dark to go get them when you really need them. You could also try drinking some of your vitamins in a health drink. Visit **http://TheHappysun.com/Vemma** for more information.

During the fall, do some proactive cooking and freeze some meals ahead for the coming winter. Stock up on some of those basic household necessities so that you can minimize your store trips in the winter. Do what you can to minimize your winter obligations so you can hibernate a little bit.

6. Set yourself up to realistically follow your treatments.

Light therapy helps. Keep a light box in an area that you are most likely to use it. This might mean having more than one type of light box. Try a dawn simulator as your alarm clock. Use a light box that looks like a desk lamp in your office. Let's face it: If it is not convenient, you will not likely use it. Winter makes us lazy like that. It might cost a little bit more to set ourselves up with the right tools, but this is a survival guide, after all, and your quality of life is worth it.

New Year's Day is really not an ideal time to start a new health routine if you have Seasonal Affective Disorder, but you should aim to at least try to walk 20 minutes per day. Use the first day of spring as a more realistic goal-setting opportunity, especially for weight- and diet-oriented goals.

A simple 20-minute walk on a treadmill is extremely helpful in releasing positive brain chemicals called beta endorphins. Find a way to make even a little bit of exercise a priority in your day. Once you actually start moving you might even find yourself motivated to do more, but the tough part is getting started and remaining consistent.

Take your supplements. 5-HTP can make a real difference in how you feel. It provides the raw material for your brain to build serotonin naturally. You are probably deficient in vitamins D and B also.

7. We are motivated to change when we are uncomfortable.

We are motivated to change when we are uncomfortable. We become driven to find answers to our problems. Perhaps we try some of those solutions and they start to work. When we start feeling good, we become a little bit more complacent in our actions and, in turn, end up sliding backwards a bit. It is human nature. When you start feeling better, try to be consistent and continue doing what is helping you.

It really is the combination of our little efforts that can help us feel better. We often look for new information or a new fad solution to our problem and dismiss the proven solutions given to us. Small consistent actions are they key to maintain our health.

8. Stop being a perfect bandwagon hopper.

We read books and buy products to help us find solutions to problems. We follow diets with strange rules and specifically regimented exercise routines ... for a while anyway, and then we stop. Maybe it is because we broke a sacred rule in the expensive plan we just paid for ... maybe we simply got bored ... maybe we made a little progress and were no longer uncomfortable. Whatever the reason, we need to stop being perfectionists and stop hopping on and off of bandwagons. When you hop off a bandwagon, you get left on the side of the road instead of moving forward.

The goal is to manage your Seasonal Affective Disorder symptoms. Don't become a *"light therapy drop-out"* simply because you missed a week. Make a YOU-turn when possible. Be a moth and return to the light. Think of your treatment options as a toolkit and not a bandwagon.

9. Let the music move you.

Here is your permission to buy something ... music. Music has a powerful effect on us. It can help elevate your mood. It can motivate you to get moving. If you do not already own one, invest in a portable music device. I am giving you permission to update your playlist with a few good songs to keep you moving in the winter.

Imagine that it is a warm summer day and you are driving down the road with the windows open. What songs are on the radio? Add the happy ones to your playlist now and listen to your music daily. Keep away from purchasing the depressing love-lost tear-jerker type songs, though, and focus on happy music.

10.Try to budget in some travel to warm sunny places.

I realize that traveling to a sunny location is not always a realistic option if you are on a tight budget. I would rather ensure that you have a light box and a few good tunes first. There are some ways to travel cheaply if you are creative. Many airlines offer credit cards that allow you to earn miles for dollars spent. If you use them responsibly to pay for your regular purchases, you can add up enough points for an inexpensive winter getaway. You need to sun to make vitamin D. Even though your health insurance won't cover the trip, the sun is therapy for Seasonal Affective Disorder. We are basically suffering withdrawal symptoms from lack of sunlight.

11. Consider a lifestyle change.

Is it possible for you to move south? Moving closer to the equator does help with SAD.

Realizing that my son was also suffering from SAD was a motivating factor for my family to move to a more southern climate. After years of feeling stuck and suffering with my own Seasonal Affective Disorder, a new job opportunity presented itself. I wanted to save my son from the depression that I desperately struggled with year after year.

We uprooted our family and moved south. It was a difficult decision, because we were leaving both of our extended families behind. We owned a house and the kids had already begun school. There were many reasons to stay up north, but the quality of life improved drastically for our family when we moved. I smile when I am outside walking on mild January day, and my friends up north are posting blizzard pictures on Facebook.

If that is too drastic of a solution, perhaps a job change with more flexibility could be an option. There are many jobs that allow you to telecommute. This might allow you to drive to a warmer climate for a few weeks or simply work from home during the winter.

While these might seem like drastic solutions, we only have one life to live. I am not advocating frivolously quitting your job and moving south without a plan. Sometimes, however, there are choices we have not even really considered, but that might improve our well-being. We are each personally responsible to consider best lifestyle options for ourselves and our families.

12. Find Support

Try to educate friends and family about your Seasonal Affective Disorder, but realize that not all of them might be supportive. Finding support and understanding is important. You might choose to work with an individual therapist or counselor. There are even counselors who can work with you over the Internet via Skype, or via other means, so you can stay warm at home instead of traveling to an office. You might also find an online support group for Seasonal Affective Disorder. Whether it is friends, family, or professional counseling, establishing a good support system is helpful.

13. Stop searching and start doing.

You already have most of the answers you need regarding treating your Seasonal Affective Disorder. Yet for some reason we feel the need to keep searching for more answers. I know. I have spent my life searching in hopes that I would discover something different to fix how I felt. I saw many of the same answers over and over again, mostly because they work. At some point, we need to focus a little less on searching, and little more on doing.

It is difficult to be consistent. Once we start feel a little better, we are less inclined to continue with the treatments that work for us. We get too busy to exercise, stop taking our supplements, and forget about light therapy. We then crash and burn and start searching again, meanwhile proclaiming that none of it works.

There is a part of us that likes the roller coaster ride and that likes the hunt. It is human nature.

We do need to try to spend a little less time searching and a little more time doing. Sit in front of your light, take your supplements and exercise so you can function as a human being. I know consistency is boring, but it is important. Use your new found health to find something more exciting to do in your life. We all need something to feel alive about. Explore and find something you can be passionate about.

14. Find the humor.

Laughter is healing. Focus your thoughts on positive and funny things. It is contagious. Watch a funny movie. Call an old friend and relive a funny incident you both shared. Spread some sunshine into other people's lives with your smile and laugh. Find the humor in dealing with Seasonal Affective Disorder.

Follow the fun on Facebook on our *You Might Have Seasonal Affective Disorder* if Facebook page at

http://Facebook.com/YouMightHaveSeasonalAffectiveDisorderif.

15. There isn't really a cure for Seasonal Affective Disorder.

Having Seasonal Affective Disorder is how certain people are hardwired biologically. It is like being a sugar maple tree whose leaves change colors with the seasons. Pine trees might try to reason with sugar maple trees and that tell them that their leaves should be green all year long and that they should not be so dramatic changing their leaves all different colors. A sugar maple tree might hate that it behaves this way and wonder why it can't control its leaves any better.

You can't really "cure" a sugar maple tree from being a sugar maple tree. The best it can do is live in a greenhouse and do "light therapy" to keep try to keep its leaves green during the winter. Some extra fertilizer or supplements might help the sugar maple through the winter as well, but ultimately the lack of sunlight will make a sugar maple tree loose it's leaves.

I hope you realize that this book is not about following the perfect treatment plan, but rather it is a place of understanding. There is no bandwagon to jump on or off here. The same treatment approach might not work for everyone, and that difference should be respected. The decisions and choices of your life are yours to make. The goal is to simply provide you with hope and empower you with options!

There isn't really a cure for Seasonal Affective Disorder. We are simply trying to manage it ... *since humans shouldn't hibernate.*

References

Introduction

National Suicide Prevention Lifeline. Call 1-800-273-TALK (8255). Retrieved July 15, 2015 from http://www.suicidepreventionlifeline.org.

What is Seasonal Affective Disorder?

American Psychiatric Association. *The Diagnostic and Statistical Manual of Mental Disorders* (4th ed., text rev.). Washington, DC: 2000.

Merriam-Webster Online Dictionary. Seasonal Affective Disorder. Retrieved July 15, 2015 from http://www.merriam-webster.com/dictionary/seasonal%20affective%20disorder.

Jamison, KR. Mood disorders and patterns of creativity in British writers and artists. *Psychiatry.*

1989;52:125–134. Retrieved from
http://www.ncbi.nlm.nih.gov/pubmed/2734415.

The Who, When, and Where of Seasonal Affective Disorder

The Who. "Behind Blue Eyes." *Who's Next.* 1971

American Academy of Family Physicians. Information from your family doctor: Seasonal Affective Disorder. *Am Fam Physician.* 2000;61:1531–1532. Retrieved from
http://www.aafp.org/afp/2000/0301/p1531.html.

World Population. Wikipedia: The Free Encyclopedia. Wikimedia Foundation, Inc.: 2015. Retrieved from
http://en.wikipedia.org/wiki/World_population.

Magnusson A, Partonen T. The diagnosis, symptomatology, and edipemiology of seasonal affective disorder. *CNS Spectr.* 2005;10:625–634. Retrieved from
http://journals.cambridge.org/action/displayAbstract?fromPage=online&aid=8889650&fileId=S1092852900019593.

Levitan RD, Massellis M, Lam RW, et al. Childhood inattention and dysphoria and adult obesity associated with the dopamine D4 receptor gene in overeating women with seasonal affective disorder. *Neuropsychopharmacology.* 2004;29:179–186. Retrieved from
http://europepmc.org/abstract/med/14560322.

Borchard T. 10 things you should know about male depression. *Psych Central.* 2011. Retrieved on from http://psychcentral.com/blog/archives/2011/05/23/1 0-things-you-should-know-about-male-depression.

Kraft U. Lighten Up: Seasonal affective disorder—the winter blues—can be lifted with bright light, as long as the treatment is timed properly. *Scientific American.* 2005. Retrieved from http://www.scientificamerican.com/article/lighten-up/.

Sher L. Genetic studies of seasonal affective disorder and seasonality. *Compr Psychiatry.* 2001;42:105–110. Retrieved from http://www.ncbi.nlm.nih.gov/pubmed/11244145.

BlankMap-World-v2. Wikimedia Commons: 2014. Retrieved from http://commons.wikimedia.org/wiki/File:BlankMap-World-v2.png#/media/File:BlankMap-World-v2.png.

Rosenthal N. *Winter Blues: Everything you Need to Know to Beat Seasonal Affective Disorder* (Revised Edition). New York, NY: The Guilford Press, 2007.

Whitehead, B. *Winter Seasonal Affective Disorder: A Global, Biocultural Perspective.* 2004. Retrieved from http://anthropology.ua.edu/bindon/ant570/Papers/Whitehead.pdf.

Why Do I Have Seasonal Affective Disorder?

Vector - Depression. 2015. Copyright: Retrieved from http://www.123rf.com/profile_joshyabb.

Vector Day Night Yin Yang. 2015. Copyright: Retrieved from http://www.123rf.com/profile_konanai.

National Institute of General Medical Sciences. *Circadian Rhythm Facts Sheet*. 2011. Retrieved from http://www.nigms.nih.gov/education/pages/factshee t_circadianrhythms.aspx.

European College of Neuropsychopharmacology (ECNP). 2014. Biochemical cause of seasonal depression (SAD) confirmed by researchers. *ScienceDaily*. Retrieved from www.sciencedaily.com/releases/2014/10/1410202124 12.htm

University of Virginia. Seasonal affective disorder may be linked to genetic mutation, study suggests. *Science Daily*. 2008. Retrieved from http://www.sciencedaily.com/releases/2008/11/0811 03130931.htm.

Lokhorst, GJ. "Descartes and the Pineal Gland," in *The Stanford Encyclopedia of Philosophy. 2015. Retrieved from http://plato.stanford.edu/archives/sum2015/entries /pineal-gland.*

Young, SN. How to increase serotonin in the human brain without drugs. *J Psychiatry & Neurosci*. 2007;32:394–399. Retrieved from http://www.ncbi.nlm.nih.gov/pmc/articles/PMC2077 351.

Murray, M. *5-HTP: The Natural Way to Overcome Depression, Obesity, and Insomnia.* New York, NY: Bantam Books, 1998.

Ross, J. *The Mood Cure The 4 Step Program to Take Charge of Your Emotions—Today.* New York, NY: Penguin Books, 2003.

Naturally SAD: Environmental Factors

Denissen, JJ, Butalid L, Penke L, et al. The effects of weather on daily mood: A multilevel approach. Emotion. 2008;8:662–667. Retrieved from http://www.ncbi.nlm.nih.gov/pubmed/18837616.

Fusani L, Coccon F, Rojas Mora A, and Goymann W. Melatonin reduces migratory restlessness in *Sylvia* warblers during autumnal migration. *Frontiers in Zoology.* 2013;10:1–8. Retrieved from http://www.frontiersinzoology.com/content/10/1/79.

Zucker I. Pineal gland influences period of circannual rhythms of ground squirrels. *Am J Physiol.* 1985;249:R111-115. Retrieved from http://www.ncbi.nlm.nih.gov/pubmed/4014491.

Other Conditions Related to SAD

Orenstein B. When summer makes you SAD. 2011. Retrieved from http://www.everdayhealth.com/depression/when-summer-makes-you-sad.aspx.

Gaines Lewis J. Reverse Seasonal Affective Disorder: SAD in the summer. *Psychology Today.* 2015. Retrieved from https://www.psychologytoday.com/blog/brain-babble/201501/reverse-seasonal-affective-disorder-sad-in-the-summer.

American Psychiatric Association. *The Diagnostic and Statistical Manual of Mental Disorders* (5th ed.). Washington, DC: 2013.

Miklowitz DJ. *The Bipolar Disorder Survival Guide: What you and your family need to know.* 2nd Edition. New York, NY: The Guilford Press, 2011.

Amen D. *Healing ADD: The Breakthrough Program That Allows You to See and Heal the 6 Types of ADD.* New York, NY: The Berkley Publishing Group, 2001.

Levitan RD, Massellis M, Lam RW, et al. Childhood inattention and dysphoria and adult obesity associated with the dopamine D4 receptor gene in overeating women with seasonal affective disorder. *Neuropsychopharmacology.* 2004;29:179-186. Retrieved from http://europepmc.org/abstract/med/14560322.

Lurie SJ, Gawinski B, Pierce D, et al. Seasonal affective disorder. *Am Fam Physician.* 2006;74:1521–1524. Retrieved from http://www.aafp.org/afp/2006/1101/p1521.html.

University of Rochester Medical Center. Getting SAD is more than having the blues. 2007. Retrieved from http://www.urmc.rochester.edu/news/story/index.cfm?id=1353.

Larson J. Seven Weeks to Sobriety. New York, NY: Ballantine Wellspring, 1997.

Raitiere MN. Clinical evidence for thyroid dysfunction in patients with seasonal affective disorder. *Psychoneuroendocrinology.* 1992;17:231–241. Retrieved from http://www.psyneuen-journal.com/article/0306-4530(92)90062-C/abstract.

Levitan R, Masellis M, Basile V, et al. The dopamine-4 receptor gene associated with binge eating and weight gain in women with seasonal affective disorder: An evolutionary perspective. *Biological Psychiatry.* 2004;56:665–669. Retrieved from http://www.ncbi.nlm.nih.gov/pubmed/15522250

The Environmental Illness Resource. Depression Seasonal Affective. 2015. Retrieved from http://www.ei-resource.org/illness-information/related-conditions/seasonal-affective-disorder/

Adventures in Light Therapy

Vector Bug. 2015. Copyright: Retrieved from http://www.123rf.com/profile_trichopcmu.

Vector Night Time Streetlamp. 2015. Copyright: Retrieved from http://www.123rf.com/profile_bigldesign.

Bright Light Lamp. Wikipedia Commons. Retrieved from https://commons.wikimedia.org/wiki/File:Bright_light_lamp.jpg.

Rosenthal N. *Winter Blues: Everything You Need to Know to Beat Seasonal Affective Disorder*. 4th ed. New York, NY: The Guilford Press, 2012.

Smith L, Elliott C. *Seasonal Affective Disorder for Dummies*. Hoboken, NJ: Wiley Publishing, Inc., 2007.

Skin Cancer Foundation. The truth about tanning in 2008. 2008. Retrieved from http://www.skincancer.org/media-and-press/Press-Release-2008/the-truth-about-tanning-in-2008.

Skin Cancer Foundation. *Skin Cancer Facts*. 2015. Retrieved from http://www.skincancer.org/skin-cancer-information/skin-cancer-facts.

PRNewswire. Light-responsive melanopsin found in many parts of the human brain. 2012. Retrieved from http://www.prnewswire.com/news-releases/light-responsive-melanopsin-found-in-many-parts-of-the-human-brain-152310145.html.

Terman M, Terman JS, Ross DC. A controlled trial of timed bright light and negative air ionization for treatment of winter depression. *Arch Gen Psychiatry*. 1998;55:875–882. Retrieved from http://www.ncbi.nlm.nih.gov/pubmed/9783557.

Skin Cancer. NCI Visuals Online. Skin Cancer Foundation. http://visualsonline.cancer.gov/about.cfm.

Vitamins, Amino Acids, and Prescription Medications

Rosenthal N. *Winter Blues: Everything You Need to Know to Beat Seasonal Affective Disorder.* 4th ed. New York, NY: The Guilford Press, 2012.

Holick M. *The Vitamin D Solution: A 3-Step Strategy to Cure Our Most Common Health Problems.* New York, NY: Hudson Street Press, 2011.

University of Maryland Medical Center. *Medical Reference Guide, Complementary and Alternative Medicine, Supplement.* S-adenosylmethionine. 2011. Retrieved from http://umm.edu/health/medical/altmed/supplement/sadenosylmethionine#ixzz3USOnLTly.

Hyman M. *Ultrametabolism: The Simple Plan for Automatic Weight Loss.* New York, NY: Atria Books, 2008.

Pöldinger W, Calanchini B, Schwarz, W. A functional-dimensional approach to depression: serotonin deficiency as a target syndrome in a comparison of 5-hydroxytryptophan and fluvoxamine. *Psychopathology.* 1991;24:53–81. Retrieved from http://www.ncbi.nlm.nih.gov/pubmed/1909444.

Selective serotonin reuptake inhibitor. *Wikipedia: The Free Encyclopedia.* Wikimedia Foundation, Inc.: 2015. Retrieved from https://en.wikipedia.org/wiki/Selective_serotonin_reuptake_inhibitor.

Weight Management for Seasonal Affective Disorder

Vector - Woman on Scale with Balloons. 2015. Copyright: Retrieved from http://www.123rf.com/profile_antimartina.

Hart C. *Secrets of Serotonin*. New York, NY: St. Martin's Press, 1996.

DesMaisons K. *Potatoes Not Prozac: Solutions for Sugar Sensitivity*. New York, NY: Simon & Schuster, 2008.

Watson B. *The Fiber 35 Diet: Nature's Weight Loss Secret*. New York, NY: Free Press, 2007.

Moving Beyond The Light

Photograph – Alone Tree. 2015. Copyright: Retrieved from: http://www.123rf.com/profile_smit

Vector- Illustrations of Various Faces. 2015. Copyright: Retrieved from http://www.123rf.com/profile_iimages

Seasonal Affective Disorder Survival Guide

Vector Holiday Health Care Stethoscope. 2015. Copyright. Retrieved from http://www.123rf.com/profile_lightwise.

INDEX

About the Author

Jozzie Ray

Born in central Massachusetts toward the end of the typewriter generation. Raised in a household that evolved from having a color television with rabbit ears to cable television with a remote control. Familiar with the less intelligent rotary phones, busy signals, and answering machine tapes. Graduated high school just as dial up internet and Prozac were becoming popular.

Initially learned about Seasonal Affective Disorder from an Oprah episode in the early 1990s and wished she had taped it on her VCR. She has spent over 25 years reading physically printed books which discuss brain chemical imbalances and a variety of other health issues. She has personally wasted thousands of dollars on gimmicks and supplements that don't work, only to diligently continue self-experimentation and finally conclude which ones may actually be effective.

She has been well schooled in the art of sarcasm, and is a "wanna-be" neurobiologist. Known for her outgoing personality, she hides her inner introvert and is actually a closet writer and poet. She can't draw or color in the lines, but is forever grateful for the invention of Photoshop so she could finally capture her imagination on paper and design this book cover.

She lives by the mantra that laughter heals, and with the heart of a child still hopes she can make a difference in this world. Happily married for over a decade and a half, and proud mother of two tween-agers who ironically are also well versed in the art of sarcasm.

She currently resides in Chesapeake, Virginia with her laptop computer, high speed internet connection, and wicked bad Boston accent. She has now finally finished writing and actually published her first book at age 39 1/2 years old ...and as a direct result of this book her house is now a total mess.

The Happy Sun

Enjoy the Book?

Find more helpful hints

on Seasonal Affective Disorder

including a

Where to Buy Guide

at

http://TheHappySun.com